PANDORA'S BOX U

A FACE FULL OF TWEETS

Facebook, Twitter and social media psyche revealed. The good, the not so good and the glamorous effects. Which Facebooker, Twitter and Selfie type are you?

BY DR SESHNI MOODLIAR

1ST EDITION

Published by
EASTERN PSYCH COURSE

Printed and bound in Poland by Kozak Druk for Dr Seshni Moodliar

A catalogue record of this book is available from the British library.
ISBN 978-0-9569941-2-7

First published in December 2014
Book for Pearls of Wisdom series
Designer: Illustrations and cover Aleksandra Rykala
Distribution: For distribution by Dr Seshni Moodliar

Contact: seshni1@hotmail.com
Cover photograph-Dr Seshni Moodliar

"We have turned our friends into an indiscriminate mass, a kind of audience or faceless public. We address ourselves not to a circle, but to a cloud…. Friendship is devolving, in other words, from a relationship to a feeling."

William Deresiewicz

"People want to share and stay connected with their friends and the people around them"; that if people have control over what they share, they will want to share more"; and that "if people shared more, the world will become more open and connected. And a world that's more open and connected is a better world."

Mark Zuckerberg

The Screenage: Generation Alpha will seamlessly interact with the world digitally. It's a world of 'Screenagers' where not only do they multi-screen and multi-task but where glass has become the new medium for content dissemination ... For Generation Alpha, glass will be all they've ever known — it won't be book or the paper, it will be glass

Mark Mccrindle

CONTENTS

DEDICATION

Thank you to God and the divine sources which make all things possible.
Thank you to my parents: Late Thirupathi Deena Moodliar, my mother
Premla Moodliar and my sisters Sanusha, Thirushna and Valashni, their
husbands and their children, Chelsea, Kyra, Anant and Arman. Thank you to
my Atha Mogie Naidoo and late Uncle Loganathan Naidoo, cousins Najen
and Devene and to the Rensburg family.

Thank you to my husband Ferdinand and my children Shreeya, Aryan and
Sitara. A hearty thank you to our families and friends in South Africa, United
Kingdom and worldwide. Special thank you our family, the Singhs and
Fredericks in England. Thank you to Pawel, staff at Kozak Druk and
Aleksandra Rykala.

My sincere gratitude to all my work colleagues, mental health professionals,
my patients and their carers. More recently those at SEPT (South Essex
Partnership Trust), Woodlea and Twinwoods Resource Centre. A special
thank you to the AMPH's (approved mental health professionals) in Milton
Keynes, Bedford and Luton. Thank you to the staff at the Starbucks, Costa
coffee, Pret, Café Nero, all the libraries and bookshops.

And last but not least thank you to all those Facebookers and non
Facebookers, tweeters and non-tweeters and other social network sites. Thank
you to all those who shared their personal stories with me.

My gratitude and thank you to all those that contributed to compiling this
book. I am so grateful and appreciative for all the support and guidance.

INTRODUCTION

Reasons for writing this book.

"The greatest discovery in life is that a person can change his future by merely changing his attitude."

Oprah Winfrey

I started researching on social networking when I was working at child and adolescent psychiatry and later in addictions psychiatry. Being someone who was a social networker, I started to realise that there was more to just my logging on daily. It was affecting me in a way which seemed to transgress in every aspect of my life– family, friendships, relationships, work, social and the core essence of my being.

I was seeing and continued to see people on a daily basis affected by Facebook and Twitter either at hospital, in the media or heard of stories from friends, relatives and colleagues. It dawned on me, that if I was seeing only a handful of people in just one town, and on a daily basis, that there must be so many other people who were experiencing the effects of these social networks worldwide.

One of the turning points for me and in a sense a reality check was when I started to regularly see teenagers who had taken overdoses, self-harmed or when I heard that someone committed suicide as a result of their Facebook posts, cyberbullying and relationships which ended because of infidelity caused by Facebook and Twitter.

I just found out on Facebook that my girlfriend was two timing me with my mate. That's why I took the overdose. She has now updated her facebook status and wall with photos of the both of them. To think, they did this while we were going out and it hurts to see this still going on. I feel like such a fool for trusting the both of them. I just couldn't believe that they could do this to me, and also that it's out there on Facebook for everyone to see.

Tom – U.K

I can assure you that Tom's story was just one of many relationship difficulties and infidelity that I have read about or heard about, which were caused as a result of social media. And if these effects that I was seeing in my work daily weren't already a huge concern, the concerns in the media of death threats slowly crept in. Celebrities as we know, being in the limelight, are always

8

being targeted. Now with social media at our fingertips, and available 24/7, the ability for fans to do this is becoming easier and easier.

'Just about every week, it seems there's a story about a celebrity, athlete, or politician receiving death threats on Twitter or Facebook'.

Kim Kardashian, Selena Gomez and Taylor Swift are just amongst a few celebrities who have received death threats and those who continue to be victimised and bullied.

President Barack Obama continues to get death threats via facebook, Twitter or emails. In 2012 a man was given 3 years' probation for posting on facebook that he was going to shoot the president. Few years down the line and with Obamacare in the media, he continues to get death threats. In July 2014 another man, who threatened him with videos that he put on Facebook was later arrested for this.

President Obama has warned, when you're young you make mistakes and you do some stupid stuff, be careful what you post on Facebook or Twitter, because in the YouTube age, what you do will be pulled up later somewhere in your life.

And he is as right as you will read later, that this is exactly what's happening- where your past could come out to haunt you.

Its de-ja-vu for me, as ten years later since the origins and birth of these social networks, I continue to see these effects and even more of Facebook, Twitter and other social networks, on adults and the younger generation, however its seems it's spreading like wildfire and the danger is, that it is getting out of control or has it already gotten out of control and we are so immersed in the grid that we choose to ignore these effects?

17-year-old Safiyyah Nawaz of North Carolina tweeted the following on 1/1/2014.
"This beautiful earth is now officially 2014 years old. Amazing."
Following her innocent post on January 1st, 2014, which she meant as a joke, she received 14 000 tweets of death threats and insults. Surely this is not what she expected when she posted that comment!!

She is luckily still alive, however, another cyberbullying victim was not so lucky.

In October 2014 a twitter troll, committed suicide few days after being confronted by Sky news reporters regarding the abusive tweets she was sending Madeleine McCann's family. The headlines read, "McCann troll Brenda Leyland driven to suicide by Twitter death threats."

Following the tragic death of Robin Williams on 11th August 2014, his daughter, Zelda Williams received images of his body and accusations that she caused his death on Twitter. In the midst of mourning for her father, she had to endure cyberbullying which eventually caused her to temporarily close both her Twitter and Instagram accounts.

Zelda wrote on Instagram: "I will be leaving this account for a bit, while I heal and decide if I'll be deleting it or not. In this difficult time, please try to be respectful of the accounts of myself, my family and my friends. Mining our accounts for photos of my father, or judging me on the number of them is cruel and unnecessary. There are a couple throughout, but the real private moments I shared with him were precious, quiet, and believe it or not, not full of photos or 'selfies.'"

She tweeted at the time: "I'm sorry. I should've risen above. Deleting this from my devices for a good long time, maybe forever. Time will tell. Goodbye."

Zelda Williams has since returned to twitter after quitting social media, simply tweeting "Thank you". The 25-year-old linked a quote by Harvey Fierstein on her Tumblr. It reads: "Never be bullied into silence. Never allow yourself to be made a victim. Accept no one's definition of your life; define yourself."

It's easier said than done, not to be bullied into silence, as social media makes it so easy for anyone to be a target for cyberbullying. Before the advent of social media, I don't think these were things that people had to endure, especially during times of the death of their loved ones.

Nowadays, in Twittersphere, Facebookland, YouTube era and WhatsApp, anything is possible. Apart from bullying and death threats which seems so unnecessary, celebrities are being mistaken for other celebrities' deaths. Related to this story is that so many celebrities are being mistaken for other celebrities' deaths on their Twitter accounts and they have been getting incorrect condolences and RIP (rest in peace) messages. As alarming as this sounds, it's true. A few examples of people who were affected by this are Joan Collins who was mistaken for Joan's Rivers death, Robbie Williams who was mistaken for Robbin Williams and Morgan Freeman who was mistaken for Nelson Mandela's death.

And if that's not enough to get you thinking about the many not so good effects of social media, actress of Hunger Games, Jennifer Lawrence, Mary Elizabeth Winstead, Kim Kardashian and others in September 2014 got nude photos of them leaked as a hacker managed to get into theirs and a few other celebrities ICloud account. And as you can imagine, the distribution of these via social media and twitter has been that's its spread like wildfire.

Winstead has addressed the matter on her own Twitter account, writing: "To those of you looking at photos I took with my husband years ago in the privacy of our home, hope you feel great about yourselves. Knowing those photos were deleted long ago, I can only imagine the creepy effort that went into this. Feeling for everyone who got hacked."

Winstead later added that she would be taking a break from social media, remarking that it was "a great day for the block button" and adding that her at-replies offer "a glimpse of what it's like to be a woman who speaks up about anything on Twitter".

Yes, dear reader, I could probably list thousands of similar stories of how social media is affecting each of us on a daily basis, irrespective of whether you're a celebrity or not. These examples you have read, are only a few that we are seeing. As a consequence of these coming to light, we are also seeing that people are being warned indirectly about the effects of social networks as it continues to make headlines and affect people's lives, but yet despite this, there continues to be a surge in users globally.

"All human actions have one or more of these seven causes: chance, nature, compulsions, habit, reason, passion, desire."

Aristotle

It's seems that using social network is the 'in thing' and that everywhere you look, it's there. The one goal for writing this is to illustrate that we are definitely becoming increasingly dependent on these social networks whether we choose to accept it or not. The new buzz words which best describe the reality of our use, whether we want to accept it or not, are the new crazed obsession of taking Selfies or Selfitis, Fear of missing out (FOMO), Whatsappatitis and Twittourettes, to name but a few.

The more addictive effects of concern are Facebook addiction disorder (FAD), Facebook depression (FD), Twitter addiction, social network dependence syndrome and divided attention disorder (DAD).

Yes, you might think that addiction is a harsh word and most might be saying as you read this, or speak about this, say that I'm not addicted...

No I am NOT addicted!!!

How do you explain this...?
"I am at work, and to be honest, all I do is spend every free minute I have on Facebook and Twitter. I don't end up finishing what I need to, but at least I know what's going on Facebook and keep up to date with my tweets. I sometimes get bored and if I wanna take a break I will just check what's going on. Other times I play games, or send messages to my mates and family. I don't think I can live without it. I have family in Italy and it's a great way to keep in touch with them too."

Luigi

This story is but one of millions of people on this earth who are doing exactly the same; checking their gadgets compulsively to browse, surf, update and check their social media accounts. As you will read later, there's instant feedback to these activities and therefore it's so easy to being addicted and distracted by the rings, dings and pings of our mobiles, iPads and computers. The truth of the matter is that the bitter pill people are choosing to swallow is that of addiction.

It's becoming more and more a reality that people are addicted to social media. As you read this and if you are not still not convinced that these exist or that yours, your relative, child or friends use of social media is becoming a problem, then I urge you to read the list of Facebook, Twitter and Selfie types which I have included later on. There's no doubt in my mind that social networks have become an integral part of our lives, but to what extent and means. I am hoping that by the end of reading this book, you would have understood the impact social networks are having on us and even more so on the younger generation-which is the grave area of concern as recently even UK super nanny Jo Frost has recently warned families with children.

On 11th September 2014, Jo Frost, super nanny has warned that social media is tearing families apart. According to her, social media is fuelling narcissistic behaviour among teenagers. She explained that the present generation of young people are growing up not being able to communicate with their parents while inhabiting a materialistic online world full of half-truths and body image paranoia. Meanwhile parents are struggling to cope with economic downturn, leaving them constantly worried about money. She says from what she sees in lots of families, the biggest problem is the negative impact and negative influence that social media is having on them.

She says that social media creates an addictive nature as teenagers become dependent on their phones which has led to the effect of breaking strong communication and relationships with family and friends.

And she is right, as you will read later, about the negative impact that social media is having. It is definitely having an impact, but we also need to understand the reason why social media is having this huge impact, and even more so on the younger generations. It's because of the times they are born in. We have all had to adapt to changes in technology however, the effects of addiction and difficulties are being seen more and more commonly in the younger generations due to them being offspring from Generation Y and Z, the post internet generations and soon to be Generation alpha, **"the glass generation"**. Read on to find out more about the different generations.

CHAPTER ONE
The Generations
Greatest, X, Y, Z and alpha

"Do you believe in the right place, right person and the right time?"

Michael Keppel

I surely believe this to be true, and as we see that Mark Zuckerberg and Jack Dorsey's inventions have peaked popularity, due to the opportunistic timing and the generations they have tapped into and are influencing.

There is much more to these social networks than we realize or want to accept, and an understanding of these generations are pivotal in understanding each of us, as individuals, our families, our children and the future generations to come. As challenging as it is, we have to grasp the understanding that we are all born in different generations with different digital age influences.

The earlier and older generations were the **Greatest Generation** which were the people who were born during the period 1901 to 1943, **Baby Boomers**, those that were born between 1943 to 1964, and **Generation X,** those that were born from 1963 to 1980's. Being the generations that were the 'pre-internet' generations means that they did not have much influence of technology on their daily lives. During those times, there were no such things as using email, internet and social network.

The **greatest generation** was characterised by the advent of the radio and television. The **baby boomers** were known as the 'me generation' and had even more influence of the television. Later on the, the **Generation X** or the 'latchkey' children became the first generation to embrace the personal computer and internet.

"I was born in the times when there was no internet. The way we communicated was different from how I see my children and grandchildren communicating. I used to enjoy making phone calls, visiting people and writing letters. That doesn't seem to be what people are doing today. When we have family home for special occasions, they spend most of the time on their phones or iPad. I don't understand technology and probably will never be able to. They seem so happy on their phone and iPads and it's quite obvious that the good old days have changed, that is, of having parties with people talking to one another, and not just on their phones. Gone are those days of just calling someone and meeting them for coffee; now they have to

let us know what's happening by posting their photos on their Facebook and Twitter accounts. I have told my children that I am old fashioned and I want to remain like that. My husband Jim feels the same way."

Sarah – U.K

The forms of communication described by Sarah, has shown how our forms of communication and socialising has changed through the generations. For the newer generations, like **Generation Y or the Millennial**, those born from 1977 to 2000, like me, **Generation Z**, those born in 1995 to 2012 and the **Generation alpha,** those born from 2010 to 2014, social media plays a huge role in communication. **Generation Y** was termed the 'techno savvy generation' and the first generation to grow up with computers. Their means of communication began with the instant messaging, text, messaging, blogs and multiple player games.

Generation Z are the first generations never to have experienced the pre internet world, are the technologically focused and iPad generation. Thanks to the digital age, the effects and ramifications of technology is evident in these generations.

What's a reality nowadays for the latter generations is that from the internet and the advancements in technology which has made so many strides in the past decades and impacted so heavily on our lives, that back in the days when posting a postcard, which used to be a preferred means of communication when on holiday, now appears to be something of the past.

For the techno savvy generations, initially, connecting to the internet and email gave them the opportunity to expand their horizons. But now using Twitter, Facebook, Google and Instagram are as second nature to everyone as breathing, as it enables people to have their finger on the pulse of what's going on in the world around them, in their friend's lives, and in the lives of politicians and celebrities.

"I'm a mother of 3 children, Michael 13, Freya 11 and Thomas 8 who are from the Generation Z and who are also representative of the iPad generation. With Michael in high school all his textbooks are on the computer and I'm struggling because you can open a book, you can smell it and put notes in the margin and they say 'Mum I don't need to'. But they

have taken it in their stride because they don't know any different.
I know that when I had homework I would go to the library with my mother and pick out books to read. Nowadays, when we sit to do homework, Michael will say all his homework is on the IPAD. If we're doing homework, they usually get distracted and check their social media accounts or instant messaging, IM. I know Michael is intelligent and he could be getting better grades, but with all these distractions, he's not studying as much. I even took him to our doctor to check if he had ADHD (Attention deficit hyperactivity disorder) or Hyperkinetic disorder, but they said he didn't have it. My kids don't want to go out with us because they would rather be at home playing games on the internet or chatting to friends on facebook and twitter. Even if they do go out, they don't seem to know how to socialise and spend most of their time on their mobiles. There seems to be something missing if I compare it to my childhood. I was happy going and doing things with my parents and the bond I had with them were strong. I am a bit worried as it's an everyday struggle now with my kids for their attention because all they want to do is be on their gadgets. When I take it away or ask for it to be put away they become upset and throw tantrums. Sometimes it's like I have to bribe them with time on their gadgets to get their homework done."

Olivia – U.K

What's being described is a shocking reality today which parents and offspring of **generation y, z and alpha** are experiencing, as we see that learning, communication and socialising has transformed drastically from the greatest generation. With technology progressing the way it has and social media being a norm for many, it's has created this illusion that it's made our lives better and easier. But if you delve deeper, there's a lot more other effects that's its having which parents are finding it more and challenging to deal with.

It's therefore not surprising then that with these advancements, "**the social media crazed generation**" are being known as the **Generation Y, Generation Z** and soon to be **Generation Alpha**.

We are indeed now so consumed with technology, that the average Briton, American or anyone for that matter, spends 8 hours or more of media from Tweeting, Facebooking, WhatsApping, using Snapshot to do internet shopping. This excludes up to 10 hours of gaming which is also part of the umbrella term, internet addiction which they all fall into. It's becoming more evident with the constant usage that it's making us slaves to its power, and in the process addicted to social media.

Leo Babauta is a well-known author and blogger of Zen habits. In his book, Focus, a simplicity manifesto in the age of distraction, he sums up the reality for the technological advancing age we live in accurately:

We live in curious times. It's called the Age of information but in another light it can be called the Age of distraction. While humanity has never been free of distraction-from swatting bothersome gnats around the fireplace to dealing with piles of paper mail and ringing telephones-never have the distractions been so voluminous, so overwhelming, so intense, and as persistent as they are now. Ringing phones are one thing, but email notifications, Twitter and Facebook message, an array of browser tabs open, and mobile devices that are always on and always beeping are quite another. More and more, we are connected, we are up to our necks in the stream of information, we are in the crossfire of the battle for our attention, and we are engaged in a harrying blur of multitasking activity.

And he is right, as you will read later, the reality for us now and the younger generations as we continue to use social media are as Leo has said, the Age of distraction and multitasking. This leads us to the prediction for **Generation alpha** by social researcher Mark Mcrindle which is that they will be a totally digitally wired-up generation, expecting connectivity on demand. If he is right, then this means that we will be connected 24 hours and 7 days a week to our gadgets. I'm not sure if any of you reading this, think this is a good thing or not and if we should be concerned about being gadgeted 24/7.

Mark Mcrindle's article: The Guardian headlines in September this year read the following:

The Screenage: Generation Alpha will seamlessly interact with the world digitally. It's a world of 'Screenagers' where not only do they multi-screen and multi-task but where glass has become the new medium for content dissemination. For Generation Alpha, glass will be all they've ever known — it won't be book or the paper, it will be glass. Together with Generation Z they will be known as "generation glass" because they will read and learn from electronic devices rather than novels and textbooks. Generation Alpha were born into a world of iPhones, YouTube and Instagram.

And we see that his predictions are slowly becoming a reality. If he is right, then, then we are going to see more and more young children of these generations hooked on gadgets because of the communication that they are used to. The reality then, is that as they continue to engage and interact online, then internet addiction (IA) and social media addiction are going to continue to pose some difficulties whether we choose to accept it or not.

WHICH GENERATION ARE YOU?

• **Greatest Generation (people born from 1901 to 1943)**
Known as the silent generation or traditionalist or radio babies. Period characterised by the advent of television and the telephone.

• **Baby boomers (people born from 1943 to 1964)**
Known as the 'me generation' or television generation.

• **Generation X (born 1963-1980)**
Known as the Latchkey kids as they were street smart but isolated.
The first generation to embrace the personal computer and internet.

• **Generation Y or Millennial-(born 1977-2000)**
Known as technological savvy generation. They were the first to grow up with computers. Their world has always had computers. The first generation to use interactive media instant messaging, text, messaging, blogs, and multi-player games.

• **Generation Z (born 1995-2012)**
First generation never to experience the pre internet world. Technologically focused and iPad generation.

• **Generation Alpha (born 2010)**
Google kids who use toys that require electric or batteries. The prediction for this generation is that they will be digitally wired up requiring 24/7 connectivity and known as the glass generation and screenagers.

CHAPTER TWO

What is social media?

There is all this hype with social media, and people continue to tweet away, not even actual knowing what it is they are using. So much so, that using **social media** has definitely changed the way we communicate and socialising. In essence, it has directly and indirectly affecting all facets of our lives, however more so on the newer Generations which these inventions coincided with.

Facebook, Twitter, WhatsApp, Bebo, Myspace, Instagram, Snapshot, YouTube and Ello, the social media newbie, all fall into this umbrella term called social media. Social media is a phrase that is being tossed around these days, which in simple terms means an instrument that is used for social communication.

"It is an interaction among people in which they create, share, and or exchange information and ideas in virtual communities."

Andreas Kaplan

Taking a closer look at Facebook and, as the name suggests, it is in simple terms…a book of faces! That's actually how it originated on a university in Harvard. It is therefore something that can be compared to an online library with names, pictures and various other information about people you know, would like to know or have known at some point in your life.

Twitter on the other hand, by prodigy, Jack Dorsey is a social networking and microblogging service that enables users to send and read texts messages called 'tweets'. Tweets are text messages limited to 140 characters.

According to Mark Zuckerberg, Facebook was built around a few simple ideas. Before he even came up with facebook, Mark Zuckerberg wrote this on his Angelfire post when he was 15 yrs. old.

"As of now, the web is pretty small. Hopefully, it will grow into a larger web. This is one of the few applets that require your participation to work well. If your name is already on The Web because someone else has chosen to be linked to you, then you may choose two additional people to be linked with. Otherwise, if you see someone who you know and would like to be linked with but your name is not already on The Web, then you can contact me and I will link that person to you and put you on The Web. If you do not

know anyone on **The Web**, *contact me anyway and I will put you on it.*"

And hey presto, few years later, here's his reasoning behind creating facebook, one of the applets which he was already planning to connect people on the web...

"People wanted to share and stay connected with their friends, and people all around them. If people have control over what they share, they will share more and the world will become more open and connected. A world that is more open and connected is a better world.

When I made Facebook, my goal was to help people understand what was going on in their world a little better. I wanted to create an environment where people could share whatever information they wanted, but also have control over whom they shared that information with. I think a lot of the success we've seen is because of these basic principles.

We made the site so that all of our members are a part of smaller networks like schools, companies or regions, so you can only see the profiles of people who are in your networks and your friends. We did this to make sure you could share information with the people you care about. This is the same reason we have built extensive privacy settings — to give you even more control over who you share your information with."

Yes, he has certainly created something which people can connect with worldwide, but at the cost of the users privacy as despite the privacy settings, what you do every day, every minute, every second is no longer private and everyone gets to see, share and have a say in your world and your life-whether you want it or not, as you continue to choose to log on to social media, you are unfortunately taking away that privilege of your privacy.

"My partner of 9 years saw a facebook picture of where I was and said I lied because the photo my mate posted showed that I was playing poker. I have tried to explain to her that it was not what it seemed on the photograph, but she has clearly said it's over. I didn't even know that my mate would put that photo up on Facebook and tag me in. I never gave him permission to do that, but I guess that doesn't matter. My partner has kicked me out of the house. I have nowhere to go and I am depressed. I just feel like dying and

23

threatened to hurt myself earlier today which is why the police have picked me up and took me to hospital. I do spend a fair bit of time on Facebook. I have some health issues, so I spend a lot of time at home. My life's been turned upside down because of one photo. What do I do now?"

Brian – U.K

"I am not sure where to begin. My partner and I split up, and I had written some personal emails about stuff that was happening to me at work. She was the only person who knew about these emails. When we split up, and in a revenge attack on me she posted these on my facebook account. I was so shocked and was bombarded by messages from a lot of people. My work found out about these emails and I was fired after a disciplinary hearing. My life has changed after one posting from my ex. I felt so helpless, and didn't get any support from anyone, despite me contacting the helpline. I am not able to work yet and it's put a strain on my life in general. I don't know what to do next."

Adam – U.K

Like in Brian's and Adam's story, more and more people are seeing, that despite the privacy settings on social media, your life is no longer private. You cannot control who posts up those drunk, naked, innocent photos or selfies.

A blog writer, Adam Clarke, has predicted that ultimately it will be Facebook, Twitter, or something else similar that will connect us and control the internet. His feelings were that Facebook, at present wants to be the thread that connects us all. And if we look at Zuckerberg's post on Angelfire when he was 15 years old, I am not surprised with this prediction. I wonder now, looking ten years down the line since the creation of Facebook, whether most people, and ardent followers, would feel that Zuckerburg has been successful?

Yes, in one sense he has been successful in connecting people worldwide, but the million dollar question is that, has this contributed to us living in a better world? Looking at all the good and not so good effects that have transpired from using it, are we sure that we want to continue to place our fate in social media to control our lives and in the lives of our loved ones for the next decade?

Jack Dorsey, Twitter prodigy, cleverly used microblogging to create a social network, which, if we thought Facebook was fast, then we were mistaken. The Twitter bug, seemed to have taken over in some aspects, and Facebook is still the lead in others.

JACK DORSEY'S STORY
Dorsey came up with this idea: 'What if you could share your status with all your friends really easily, so they know what you're doing? Within two weeks, Dorsey had built a simple site where users could instantly post short messages of 140 characters or less, known in Twitter parlance as "tweets". On March 21, 2006, Jack Dorsey posted the world's first tweet: "just setting up my twitter'.

Coincidentally according to him, his three key reasons for Twitters success was:
1. Initially writing his idea out.
2. Making use of opportunistic timing.
3. Taking feedback and refining his idea.

He definitely made use of opportunistic timing, but when he refined his idea, did he predict the twitter trolls, cyberbullying, stalking and other effects that have transpired from people tweeting?

Yes, dear reader, tweeter or non-tweeter, Facebooker or not a Facebooker, generation x, y and z, it was therefore the totally right, perfect and opportunistic timing for him and Zuckerberg as they tapped into the generations they have. A recent estimate is that Twitter users tweet 400 million times a day, whilst Facebook processes over 500 terabytes of new data every single day, so it's therefore not surprising to its popularity.

There are some similarities and some distinct differences between these network sites, and others like Snapshot, Bebo, Myspace and WhatsApp. However, they are all working in the same way.

In a more advanced way of looking at it, as you will read later, they have managed to tap into not only our lives, but the very core essence of our being and our brain or 'Connectome', as research on the human Connectome project explores these intricate network of connections in our brain in detail of which

I will explain later.

Nowadays, people use social networks to update their profiles with status updates and tweets, and in essence, are using these social networks as virtual diaries to record their lives. These details are then available to those whom they choose to allow to view them. As you will read later, it's fantastic to have this opportunity to have a virtual diary, but at what cost?

We are calling it social network and we are socialising in a virtual world and on screens. Isn't socialising supposed to be face to face contact and being physically present with people? How can we say we are socialising when we send someone a message, smiley or poke or tweet them? They are not real interactions. We are in contact yes, and in some sort of communication. But surely, our day to day socialising and connecting physically with people is better that tweeting, WhatsApping, snapshotting, than actually going out with someone.

Social networks are on the rise and people are beginning to place a lot of emphasis on it. And if you thought Facebook and Twitter were the only social network sites, there are many others that are on the increase including WhatsApp.

In September 2014 the top ranked social network sites are:
Facebook
Twitter
LinkedIn
Pintinterest
Google
Tumblr
VK
Flick
Vine
Meetup
Tagged
Askfm

Meetme
Classmate

Well, watch this space as newbie and top secret Ello might be going on the list too. Ello was created by Paul Budnitz, a bicycle shop owner, is by invite only and has the following manifesto:

"Your social network is owned by advertisers. Every post you share, every friend you make and every link you follow is tracked, recorded and converted into data. Advertisers buy your data so they can show you more ads. You are the product that's bought and sold.

We believe there is a better way. We believe in audacity. We believe in beauty, simplicity and transparency. We believe that the people who make things and the people who use them should be in partnership. We believe a social network can be a tool for empowerment. Not a tool to deceive, coerce and manipulate — but a place to connect, create and celebrate life. You are not a product."

They may have a point, that all your data is being recorded as writer Adam Clarke alluded in one of his blog posts that everything is being recorded by Facebook and by some high tech means as well, which Facebook had declined to comment on. You don't realise it, but it's true, that your every move is being tracked, recorded and converted into data. When you sign up to these networks, do they tell us this is what's going to be done or is it just understood, that we are signing away our privacy, and agreeing to be spied on.

The future predictions are that we are not going to just use social media as our virtual diaries but for Omni channelling. Omni channelling is being promoted for business globally to enable the realisation of social business. Which means that social media will not only be for socialising but for also running our day to day lives and shopping all built in one. Looks like it's headed that way with businesses, communities, schools, institutions all wanting to be on these networks. At what cost though?

The future prediction by the American Council for Civil Liberties sees that someone may phone up to buy a pizza, and the order-taker's computer gives her access to your voting record, employment history, library loans — all "just wired into the system" for your convenience. She'll suggest a tofu pizza as she knows about your 42inch waist, she'll add a delivery surcharge because a nearby robbery yesterday puts you in "an orange zone" — and she'll be on her guard because you've checked out the library book Dealing With Depression and watched its pizza video online.

This is not too hard to believe that this could be the way technology is moving in the future, especially if Omni channelling is on the horizon. This could affect our daily lives and in fact control it. Are we prepared for that prospect? With social media use and having all our details at their fingertips, they could do whatever they want to and sell it to whomever they want to as long as we continue to be players in their game.

CHAPTER THREE

"To be or not to be, that is the question."
William Shakespeare

To be or not to be on Facebook or Twitter or maybe Ello, that is still the burning question nowadays. There are reminders everywhere we go, what we see, what we hear, and this has crept into every aspect imaginable in our very existence. It seems no doubt, that whether you are a loyal follower or not, there is no escaping the effects of these social networks.

I imagine, that wherever you are, and wherever you are reading this, whether you are on a vacation in Spain, in an underground in London, in Africa or India, or Poland and China, 'to be or not to be on Facebook or Twitter' is a question that either you have had first-hand experience or it is something that you know that someone else has dabbled with. Or many of you may have been on the receiving end of being asked whether you are on Facebook or Twitter.

I don't think there is a right or wrong answer here, and as you will see, nestled in these pages, I am hoping to explore the good, not so good, glamorous and not so glamorous effects of these shades of blue that has taken over our lives.

Looking into the future, I am hoping to impart some wisdom as a guidance either for you or your family members. The creation Facebook, by prodigy Mark Zuckerberg, which originated on a university campus, boasts now over 1 billion people, and if not even more, as this number increases every second of the day.

My dilemma of whether to be or not to be on social network
I got my invitation email which read:
'Dear Seshni
Dion Lakey has asked you sign up to Facebook.
Click on this link to sign up and create your user name and login.'

Initially I got this and later a twitter sign up. I was excited and like all new things wanted to know the pros and cons of signing up to Facebook and Twitter which you will read later. I must admit that I was in a bit of a dilemma as to whether I sign up or not and as to what the benefits of these new crazes where. I started to do my own bit of research and to hear stories from various people from all walks of life. Some were avid followers coercing me to sign up and others were just against social networks and refused to engage in any talk about it.

These were just some of the stories I encountered in the beginning like the following two stories of my co-workers.

"I am a nurse and single mother with 2 children. This connection gives me that contact with friends and family, especially for my kids. Also, being on my own, it's easier and more convenient for me to have this connection. As you can understand, I am not able to go out much and this is my only means of socialising. I don't feel so isolated and I am able to contact people in similar predicaments. I am also able to be in contact with other nurses and some of the psychiatrists I work with. My son is a professional skater and I use it to advertise his latest winnings. He has to go for daily training and has to have certain attire which costs a lot of money. I have also been able to raise money on Facebook for his competitions."

Louisa – U.K

Another colleague of mine, a GP turned psychiatrist, told me this when I asked him whether he was on facebook:

"I am not sure what the hype is about. Personally I don't think it's something I want to sign up to. I think the whole thing is so narcissistic. All people are doing are putting photographs of themselves which is just making them more vain and competitive. It's like how it used to be in school where people are posting photos to see who the most popular one is. And in any case why would I care what someone had for breakfast or did the night before. I don't want to become a stalker or follow people's lives and also struck off because of Facebook or Twitter. It's like you are spying on people, isn't it? I was shocked when he said but few years down the line and having experienced the effects of social media-he was right".

I was privy to both ends of the spectrum of good and not so good effects of social networks. Eventually, like many, and being an offspring from Generation Y, attempting to keep up with the times of technology and the curiosity of the unknown, I succumbed to signing up. I initially, like all Facebookers and tweeters, started logging on daily for my daily dose, enjoying the thrill of signing up 100's of friends, updating my status and posting photos. I am hoping this sounds familiar to some of you.

However, the novelty and excitement slowly wore off as I realised and started to see lots of the psychological effects that were affecting people I loved, my clients and the more and more I researched I realised that as much as there were so many wonderful features that Facebook, Twitter and social media were giving, and in the same token there were just as many reasons not to subscribe.

If you're a user of social media, does this statement resonate with you? *"Can't live with it and can't live without it."*

Personally, I found that when I first signed up to Facebook and Twitter, that the whole experience of social networking was addictive, like once you hit that subscribe button, there's no turning back-or so I thought before I considered to disconnect.

In the past, South Africa's late president Nelson Mandela's description of a typical day was a reality and this is how I envisage my days to be.
I love playing and chatting with children; feeding and putting them to bed with a little story. Being away from the family has troubled me throughout my life. I like relaxing at home, reading quietly, taking in the sweet smells coming from the pots, sitting around a table with family and taking out my wife and children. When you can no longer enjoy these simple pleasures, something valuable is taken away from your life and you feel it in your daily work."

Nelson Mandela

As you are reading this, my question to you is, how many of us can honestly say that we are living in the now as described here to enjoy the wonderful treasured and rich moments of our lives. What is a reality nowadays is that our homes and living rooms are transformed into **media hubs** with gadgets ranging from mobiles, laptops, iPads, iPods and people two-screening, texting, tweeting, WhatsApping, sexting and Facebooking....does this sound familiar? We are not able to live in the now because we are distracted by our gadgets.

Just say for example, you are sitting with your family and enjoying the movie that's playing. A ring, ding and ping later you have to answer that WhatsApp or tweet. You tell your kids, just excuse me a bit but I just have this send this quick message, text and email. Or if you are browsing on Facebook or Twitter, and your little one comments, mum or dad, can I see what you are looking on facebook.

As writer Craig Kanalley writes:
"You're waiting in line. Enter: your phone.
You're in an awkward social situation. Enter: your phone.
You're at home - bored, alone. Enter: your computer.
All of these times, you go to Facebook or Twitter."

Just think back to the last 24 hours and how many times you looked at your mobile, or either of your social network sites like Facebook and Twitter. Maybe you will admit to checking it 10, 20, 30, 50 or 100 times. Why do we feel the need to be so connected on our phones rather than just live in the moment and soak in the awareness of the sights, smells, tastes and sounds around us? Why do we feel the need to be constantly distracted by our gadgets even to the sacrifice of spending times with our loved ones?

And like Leo Babauto has described in this age of information, it's an age of distraction, where we are constantly battling for our own attention.I realised that we ultimately set an example for the younger generations and the people around us. Children are good learners and will model the behaviour they are seeing their parents or friends engaging in. It got me thinking as to what message I was sending to people around me and my kids. That it's a norm to be checking facebook, twitter and WhatsApp periodically throughout the day. That signing up 100's of friends and followers, of even people I don't know is right….. it got me thinking and that's when I considered to disconnect.

THE WINTER OF MY DISCONNECT
"I had decided to de-tech from social networks Christmas 2013, and I was hoping that I would be Facebook and Twitter free throughout Christmas day. There was not even a remote chance of this happening. Facebook and Twitter seemed to consume and own every second of our Christmas day, whether I wanted it to or not.

Our Christmas present rampage was posted within seconds of midnight thanks to the advances in our digital age. Hey presto, the rest of the country and folk in America, South Africa, India, Australia, Ireland and Scotland and virtually the rest of the world, were able to view every detail of this moment from the Christmas tree, from the roaring fire to the time the little ones opened their Christmas presents .

Later that day, at the dinner table, every few minutes of conversation was peppered by someone with a Facebook comment or tweet, thus to the extent that our lovely hostess demanded for all mobile phones to be kept off the dinner table. Two of the guests managed to continue their texting and sexting as they concealed their phones under the table, but you could still hear the fidgeting on their gadgets.

I was drawn back into a world I thought I had left behind, at least for the day, as even our conversations revolved around the current happenings on some of the guests Facebook and Twitter accounts. People were distracted and checking their accounts every five minutes, making very little eye contact.

To my surprise later that day, I was to find out that one of the friends at the table hooked up with someone via Facebook. This guy had seen her profile photo on Facebook, fancied her and then asked to meet her. It was alarm bells and not jingle bells that went off as he wanted to meet up with her at a Christmas fair in a town 2 hours away from home. She had never met him before and only knew of him through her contact with him on Facebook, but she was still eager to meet him. This was however not going to happen as her parents requested to meet him first, instead of sending their daughter off to meet a man she has never physically seen before.

Later on, even before we even began to savour the turkey roast and lavish spread of scrumptious food- every detail of our meal was instagrammed thanks to the new crazed obsession of 'food porn'.

A few days later, at the New Year's celebration at Trafalgar Square in London, things appeared to be no different, with people on their iPads and mobile phones sending tweets and updating status of the awesome firework displays and performance by Gary Barlow.

Despite being drenched with rain, this was no put off for the social media crazed generations who were missing the point of enjoying the amazing historical moment of the New Year, trading it for status updates, tweets, and almost perfect instagrammed photos and Selfies.

On my first day back to work after the Christmas break I was listening to how the radio 1 and HEART Disc jockeys (DJ's) who were talking about Facebook and Twitter and coercing listeners to tweet them about a song they would want to hear and about messages about how their New Year celebrations was.

At work, even one of my first assessments turned out to be someone with possible Asperger's syndrome, who confessed to spending every free moment on Facebook and Twitter!! It dawned upon me, that as these were only some of the examples which I was coming across, I was sure there were so many more examples illustrating the daily influences these social networks are having.

I therefore could go on and on, about the daily influences these networks have on us, but then again, if you're a loyal tweeter or Facebooker, I think you know exactly what I was experiencing. You see, whether you are at work, surfing the net, listening to the radio, reading the newspaper, at a social event, at school, college, the gym, out at a restaurant or coffee shop, or even just at home at the dinner table, the thing that's on everyone mind and that people are talking about is Facebook or Twitter or one of the other social network sites."

So, with these influences creeping up on us on a day to day basis, and alluring enticements everywhere we look, from the moment we get out of bed, till the moment we go to bed, then why is it that not everyone has succumbed to unleashing their Pandora's Box?

Why is it that 6 billion people on this earth vow not to succumb to this, as if it is like contracting a deadly disease, for fear that they will be a victim to its prey, due to lack of privacy and limitations of the ever advancing digital age.

Daniel has recently warned social media celebrities and said, 'I don't have Facebook and Twitter and I think it makes things a lot easier. If you go on Twitter and tell everybody what you are doing in that moment and then claim you want a private life, then no one is going to take your request seriously.'

There are also some who fear it like the forbidden fruit in the Garden of Eden that Eve succumbed to, like the chef Jamie Oliver, who has stopped his 11 year old daughter from using social networks, after he found out his daughters had created Instagram accounts.

Arsenal's leading goal scorer, Thierry Henry, has said that he does not approve of social media sites like twitter and Instagram. He does not understand why people use it. He says that he has no plans to use social media due to his old school ways.

He says he has a zero interest or minus 120 % interest. He is old fashioned and doesn't want to use Twitter despite his team mates being on Twitter. He says he prefers face to face contact with people rather that tweeting.

"Life is divided into three terms-that which was, which is and which will be. Let us learn from the past to profit by the present, and from the present, to live a better future."

William Wordsworth

It is becoming crystal clear, that despite huge positives that are coming out of social network, the psychological effects are more than we realise or want to accept and some wiser ones are choosing not to engage in social media. However for some, social media continues to dominate our present and will have an even bigger impact on our future. Looking into a crystal ball, Forbes' prediction for our futures of 2014 and 2015, which is not surprising, is that there is going to be more emphasis on social networking for businesses, but at the same time, more rehabilitation centres for people to lead data centric balanced lives. And more recently in August 2014 as much as social media is being used in businesses, they have warned businesses that social media is actually decreasing productivity of their employees as they continue to be distracted by these networks. So it might be omni channelling in the future, but at what costs to employees and companies.

Another prediction is as we see a boom in Facebook and Twitter graveyards  and death data advisors will be employed to go through deceased profiles. Surely, this is not what we envisage for ourselves and others, to be reduced to cyber or virtual cemeteries?

If we compare our use of social network to Pandora's box- is it still early days to know, and as to what this unleash of 'Pandora's box' has in store for us all disastrous consequences as when Pandora opened the box given by Zeus and released hate, envy, crime, and illnesses unto the world and so much chaos known to man. Or is there some hope like when Pandora realised what she had done, and then she thankfully freed hope into the world, for the future.

I guess my reader, only time will tell, but in the meantime, taking a closer look at these networks, I am hoping to reveal the good, the not so good, the glamorous and the wisdom of hope for the future for ourselves, our families and the younger generation.

As Mark Zuckerberg has said, we would be able to control what we share, or so we think, and that by doing so we are making the world a better place…or so we truly hope.

CHAPTER FOUR

Social media - The reasons why we are connecting.

"In the sweetness of friendship let there be laughter and sharing of pleasures. For in the dew of little things the heart find its morning and is refreshed."

Khalil Gibran

The Precious global Connection

Possibly the reason most people are glued to their Facebook and Twitter profiles every second of every minute of every day, is because of the connection it gives us with the rest of the world, which was Zuckerberg's original aim.

Connecting allows us to connect and form many relationships.
This is possibly one of the main reasons that we keep logging on, like moths to a flame. Social networks allow us to connect with many friends, family, groups and also provides a means to meet people. At first, with enthusiasm and optimism at its peak, you would be signing up as many people as possible, be they known, acquaintances, an ex or someone with a similar interest, and this could earn you the coveted title of being 'Mr/Ms Popular Facebooker type.'

This was a similar experience for me when I first accepted the invitation for Facebook from my friend Dione Lakey. After my in depth research into it, I was sure I was doing the right thing. I was so excited to use this new internet tool that was going to connect me with my friends, family and colleagues. I was sure that as this was the new best thing since the advent of the internet and emails. I started to add friends daily as I realised that this connection could keep me in touch with people all over the world.

And like most people, adding these friends made me feel like I was so popular so much so, that whether these were real friends or not, strong or fickle, that didn't matter. Whilst doing this, I slowly began to realise that being in the virtual world, meant that we choose to forgo having relationships which thrive on face to face contact and using all our five senses of sight, smell, touch, hearing and taste. As we choose virtual friends over real life relationships, we have chosen to rather hear tweets on our keyboards than the voice of a loved one.

The general trend with social networks is to rekindle the friendships of those who were significant ones in the past which is what I started to do. Even if they were just acquaintances, they were now my Facebook friends and people I was following on Twitter. I thought that, this was acceptable to connect with those we have known in our past.

"I don't think I want to use Facebook right now. I am too busy in my life, going out and spending time with my family. Work is busy as it is, so I am not sure where I would fit in the time to check my accounts. I have heard you sign up all your old friends and acquaintances. I have contact with few of my friends. I have always been a private person and would like to remain like that. That's all happened in the past and I think it should stay there in the past. I am sorry but I am not keen to join Facebook now."

Sasha

This got me thinking as my friend Sasha pointed this out, what if we don't want to reconnect with a certain person because of a bad experience, or an ex-boyfriend, how do we avoid signing them up? She pointed out that why would we want to invite people we left behind in our lives, back into our lives as she felt that as innocent as it was, this could cause more harm. And I guessed she was right, as despite privacy features, it was difficult to say no to people who tracked me down and requested to be a friend.

As I started to connect with people all over the world, the fantastic features of letting people know my whereabouts was pleasurable, instant and easy. That's another reason why people connect. Whether you are on a night out, at school, work, or on holiday in the Bahamas, thanks to the digital age, with one status update, selfie or tweet and hey presto, the rest of the world and your family and friends knows what you are doing.

That's the sheer beauty of these social network sites. Just the knowing that you can be in touch with the click of a button, and that you are not alone in this world. Even if we are living in a foreign country or even in the same country as our families, it gives us the opportunity to connect with them and even see them using FaceTime.

"Ayaan was admitted as an emergency to hospital with a viral infection. FaceTime was a godsend for us as my wife and I could keep in contact with each other. I had to go back to work and she was in hospital with him. Because of the hours, it was so convenient for us to contact each other. We were also able to connect with our family in India who were also worried about him. Thankfully he recovered but we are so glad we could keep in touch with our family, especially to have the support and communication during this difficult time."

Dr Solomon -U.K

As it turned out for a colleague of mine, using FaceTime was a lifesaver for a friends whose son was unexpectedly in hospital in the UK and as a result, their family in India were able to keep in touch with them.

"My Facebook story is one of success. I was adopted when I was young and through my birth mother I was able to trace my family in Australia. I have always felt there was something missing. My mother had some details of our family abroad which I used on facebook and twitter. After a few months of searching online and posting details, one of my family abroad contacted me. I was so excited and thrilled. As you can imagine I have a whole new family to meet and get to know. I am also able to have contact with them regularly on Facebook and Twitter. To think I would never have found out about them had it not been for Facebook or Twitter."

Miriam -U.K

When I started to use social media, I began to hear more and more about social network and how it had also positively influenced people's lives. Like the success story of one of the receptionists in the hospital where I worked, who told me about how through Facebook and Twitter, she was able to track down family in Sydney, Australia.

As you may be aware of, social networks does not just connect you to your family and friends whom you love and feel the need to update regularly on your whereabouts. It could be that you're in a relationship and you want your relationship and affection of love to transcend into the cyber world.

How many times have you seen the status of relationship of a person change?

Facebook status: in a relationship • ex• single • married • no status

People are starting to form relationships on Facebook and Twitter. There are young woman and girls, men and boys, who are living from tweet to dates. They are counting the hours when they can change their status and when they can start to flood Instagram with pictures of their boyfriend's eyes or girlfriends eyes hashtagged #beautiful.

How many times have you had someone comment on your profile photo and that they would like to meet up? I know I have. Gone are the days of meeting people at social gatherings, parties, clubs or outings. It's more and more common that people are just meeting each other on Facebook and Twitter and continuing their relationship using these social networks.

"My Facebook story is one of romance. A friend of my brothers saw my profile. He got in contact with me and initially I was reluctant to, but I spoke to my brother's friend who could vouch for him. We started to chat on Facebook daily and then on the phone. Later on, we started going out and we are now are officially in a relationship. I would have never thought I would meet someone on Facebook. He has come to visit me, but my parents have forbid me to go to his. He also wanted us to go for a weekend away. My parents got so worried and started to check his profile and friends he was hanging out with, just so they could find out more about him. I feel it's an invasion of my privacy and embarrassed a bit that they would do that."

Maria - U.K

"Hans and I met on the virgin clubs network. He is an instructor in Holland and I am working in a gym in UK. You know we have some group hangouts. He contacted me the one day, said he liked my profile picture and that's how it all started. I didn't think anything of it as we were colleagues and obviously knowing the distance, there wasn't any plans on my side to have a relationship or so I thought. One thing led to another, from just messaging, to tweeting and then calling each other and skyping. Strangely enough we started to date. He has surprised me with visits to the UK and I am planning to visit him in Holland. I have never been so happy in my life.

Stacy -U.K

Facebook and Twitter has also resulted in some unbelievable and romantic relationships forming as a result of networking, as I recently found out about one of the Virgin active gym instructors fairy-tale romance which started after she met him on Facebook.

On the other hand, as easy as it is to form relationships, we see that it's just as easy to defriend them, de-ex them, and block them from your profiles?

An article in the Guardian newspaper titled:
How Facebook can ruin your relationship: 'Site induced jealousy' increases risk of divorce and break-up by the following ways:
*Excessive Facebook use increases risk of cheating, break-up and divorce.
*People jealously monitor their partner's activities and reconnect with their ex.
*The younger the relationship, the greater the risk of Facebook problems.

And as much as there are fairy-tale romances that have sparked because of social media, we are also seeing the negative effects of social media on relationships.

"I am heart broken and depressed. My ex, Miguel, and I broke up a few days ago. I am devastated. He just decided that our relationship of 1 year is over. He hasn't even given me a reason. I have been looking on his Facebook and Twitter accounts and I am so gutted. I know he has moved on as I saw him with another girl on his Facebook. I even checked her profile out and who her friends are. From her posts, it seems they are

planning to go for a weekend away. I don't know for sure, but that's what her status says. Those were the things we used to love doing together. To top it all off, he has now defriended me and blocked me from his account. I am not sure how to deal with this. I can't seem to cope and that's why I have been cutting myself."

Sarah -U.K

Sarah was having an intense relationship which she thought was leading to marriage. She was left heartbroken when they broke up, but even more devastated as she found out he had defriended her. In the process, checking on her partners Facebook account was making her into a stalker.

People from all generations have been benefitting from the younger generation to even the older generations.
It has allowed for elderly people to connect with family. We know as we age, people become more isolated so it is not surprising that, according to families of the elderly, now even for them, using the internet and creating profiles, is something which is being promoted in homes and by aged care groups.

The aim is to reinvent what it is to be old, for people to stay connected to their community and family and thus removing the social isolation. Chairman of the psychogeriatric group, Marco Trabucchi, said that research shows that social networks help keep the brains of the elderly active, and stimulates their memory.

"I use my Facebook account regularly to keep in touch with my son and grandchildren in the United States. Alex is our only son and he immigrated to the states. We don't get to see them as much but using Facebook and Twitter helps us keep contact with them. It's also useful as we get to see our grandchildren whom we love and miss a lot. They also enjoy the contact we have as it keeps us connected and up to date with what's going on in their lives. We don't feel isolated as we get older, and just knowing their available to use online if we needed is helpful."

Sylvia and Dan -U.K

For the younger generation, the influences of social network are even more.

Even children at school, colleges and universities are using social media as a platform for academia, to aid with their education and extracurricular activities.

"I use Facebook to connect with my class mates, share homework and get help with my assignments. Sometimes it's not always possible in school to keep up to date with all the work, but using Facebook and Twitter helps us so that we can share our homework and remind each other. It's useful for me if I know I have forgotten something. We share notes, and discuss what we need to do for our homework. It can mean that some evenings I have to be constantly chatting to my mates. When its exam time, my mum doesn't allow me the phone, because she says it's too distracting."

Chelsea Balliram -South Africa

My niece in South Africa says she and her classmates use it for homework and I think that's the trend for most school goers and post graduates.

Apart from being connected, it is about keeping contact with those close to us, or to wanting to belong to a community or group. This cyber existence engenders a sense of community. In essence it gives us a sense of belonging. We all have the desire to belong to something and for many people it fills that void of belonging to something. You could be a normal individual or someone who has difficulty interacting with people. We all want to feel connected to people and whether it is for love or likeness, we have that ongoing desire.

It useful for people who need extra support
It's also a lifesaver for those with social phobias, anxiety or Asperger's syndrome, for whom the very thought of socializing would be virtually impossible in reality. People with illnesses and genetic disorders, use social media daily as a means of connecting with other people around the world with similar illnesses.

"My daughter Anna has Downs's syndrome. She doesn't go out all the time. She uses Facebook to connect with other people like her. I am so happy she has this because it can be isolating for her. It's no longer the case as she can now connect with other people with Down's syndrome and also some of our family and friends. She just loves it. She also uses Twitter to read up on

46

the latest news for people with Downs's syndrome. She doesn't feel so isolated. I do worry sometimes though that she can be vulnerable and not always understand what's going on with some messages and what other people are doing. Also that it can influence her in a bad way. She uses it most of the time to keep connected with friends and family and people like her. She has some part time work, and it also helped her with that."

Gabriella - U.K

"I live in Dubai. Apart from using Facebook and Twitter to connect with my family and friends in South Africa, when I found out I had SLE I was devastated and didn't know what to do. I turned to social networks because it was an easier means of communicating as to how I felt and what I was going through. Other people around me made me feel uncomfortable. I also use it to connect with people with SLE which has provided me great support. I would say I have coped better as I have been so fortunate to meet so many people like me who are going through the same thing and it just makes each day a lot easier."

Ria - Dubai

The impact of being able to connect with people from all walks of life is phenomenal and all this with just the touch a button. There is now easier access to a range of support groups for illnesses such as cancer, HIV, mental and physical illnesses and so much more.

There are many Facebook and Twitter groups, ranging from a variety of interests that people subscribe to. What better way to pursue your interests than by belonging to a group of people that share the same interests, and can provide some sort of catharsis in a sense. You can discuss hot tips, dos and don'ts of special interests. These are also fantastic features for those football fans who exchange information, thereby enriching their knowledge and making sure they have the updated information.

It's helpful for fundraising and charity events
There has even been many success stories of people raising for charity via Facebook and Twitter. Stephen Sutton was a teenager who was dying with cancer. He sadly passed away in May 2014. He raised more than £4 million

by using social media.

"Hi! My name's Stephen and I'm pretty much like your average teenager- except for the last three years now I've been battling cancer. The current opinion voiced by my doctors is that my disease is incurable, and as a result I want to spend as much time as possible raising funds for a charity very close to my heart."

Recently the ice bucket challenge had gone viral with people from all walks of life and celebrities contributing to the challenge. It was started by Corey Griffin, 27, who had helped the campaign become an internet sensation after watching his friend Peter Frates struggle with the motor neuron disease- Amyotrophic Lateral Sclerosis (ALS) . Corey Griffin has tragically died in August 2014 after drowning.

Sadly also, a young man died following his attempt of this challenge.

The death of an 18-year-old Scottish man in a flooded quarry is being linked to the "ice bucket challenge"- Cameron Lancaster, of Burntisland, FifeMan

For the so called **'social butterflies'**, social media is a dream tool, which allows people to even organise events and publicise this via the internet. Whether it be local town events, to birthday parties, fundraising and media events, this is the tool being used and in a place where people start to network socially in order to maximise the media coverage and distribution of their invitations.

We can connect and follow celebrities.
People look up to celebrities, whether it's a singer, actress, actor, author, political leader or motivational speaker- we want to follow them.

For twitter, I know it's about following your favourite star, and receiving tweets of the latest up to date info of your interests. A classic example is like recently, the long awaited wedding photo of Kim Kardashian and Kanye West on 24th of May 2014 that received 2 million likes on Twitter.

"She loves Instagram, finds Twitter fun and Facebook as a great brand builder."

Kim Kardashian

I always say I feel really bad for my little sisters," Kardashian told Entertainment Tonight of the negativity her family faces. "I would really hate for the day when my daughter North, has to get on social media, because of the comments like cyber bullying. Sometimes they can be so negative." The reality TV star, who is publishing a book of selfies, admitted that the feedback she gets on Twitter and Instagram can also "be really uplifting too." Kardashian explained that she often looks to her social media followers when she needs "motivation to work out," because they are "super positive and supportive."

The star recently lamented on Twitter that she is not as thin as she used to be. "I was needing some motivation from the Twittersphere, to help me work out a little bit harder and to get back onto my no carbs/Atkins diet," she said of the tweets. "I fell off a little bit. I just gotta get focused and get back on."

So in one sense Kim is promoting social media, but on the other hand, she is also aware of the negative effects that cyberbullying has on her family, which as you read earlier is a reality and has come at an expensive price to pay. The concerns she has raised for her daughter North is interesting, as who knows what lies in store for the Generation alphas who will be using social media.

And likewise for celebrities like Rihanna, Katy Perry, Justin Bieber and even President Barack Obama, it's about letting their fans know their whereabouts and sharing their views. What avid users don't realise that they might be taking time out in their day updating their statuses, however most celebrities and others have got social media managers who are updating their statuses. So celebrities are not necessarily as distracted using social media as the general population who use it.

We have also seen that some social media users are also becoming celebrities themselves as a result of their social media use.

We are able to connect with media.
We even see a surge in Radio and television stations all advertising on Facebook and Twitter. It is being used to promote their influence on the public and their followers. Whether it be to rate their favourite songs, radio listeners are being urged to log onto their Facebook and Twitter pages.

Social media is the ultimate dream tool for bloggers, as now with Hoot Suite, with one post it's all directed to Facebook, Pinterest and Instagram.

According to Forbes magazine, who are encouraging small businesses to use social networks, for 2014 and 2015, the prediction is that social media will become a necessity for businesses and not a luxury. Even using LinkedIn is becoming a must.

Since the advent of Facebook and Twitter, there has been many a success story of home businesses, which I have personally come across. People thriving in all facets of businesses, ranging from cakes and other food, clothing, computers and the list is endless.

This clearly illustrates the importance and impact Facebook and Twitter, amongst others, has on not only our personal lives but also on the economy and peoples professions, which inadvertently will have an impact on the health and wellbeing of each and every one of us. And for the future trends in business, social media appears to be a must. Having said that, despite this, Forbes have also warned people that using social network is also decreasing productivity of businesses.

Social media is useful for crime investigations
Police are even on social networks and consist of police stations and crime watch who are also known subscribers who are able to keep tabs on those that pose a risk to the public. With the increase in cybercrime and other criminal activities this is becoming an important area of work for the law force.

In order to solve crimes as we have seen on CSI, using people's profiles is becoming the norm as this could provide them with the clues and evidence needed in order to prosecute criminals or even monitor their activity. Some crime preventative measures are being taken up by local police authority and extensive crime watch on the internet is becoming increasingly a daily practice.

The changes in the law now meant that prisoners and inmates are allowed to have access to Facebook and create their own accounts. This particularly became a problem when inmates were able to use their smartphones to access Facebook, takes photos and also make threats to their victims.

Facebook has recently revealed its pledge to reveal all if subpoenaed. Recently Facebook has acknowledged that if subpoenaed, they would allow police access to your Facebook profile and provide them with a printout.

THE FACEBOOK PLEDGE
'We work with law enforcement where appropriate and to the extent required by law to ensure the safety of the people who use Facebook. We may disclose information pursuant to subpoenas, court orders, or other requests (including criminal and civil matters) if we have a good faith belief that the response is required by law.

This may include respecting requests from jurisdictions outside of the United States where we have a good faith belief that the response is required by law under the local laws in that jurisdiction, apply to users from that jurisdiction, and are consistent with generally accepted international standards.

We may also share information when we have a good faith belief that it is necessary to prevent fraud or other illegal activity, to prevent imminent bodily harm, or to protect ourselves and you from people violating our Statement of Rights and Responsibilities. This may include sharing information with other companies, lawyers, courts or other government entities.'

Yes as you see, there are so many wonderful reasons to keep us logging on, but despite that there are still those who fear this connection and who have vowed not to succumb to social networks?

SUMMARY OF REASONS WHY PEOPLE ARE CONNECTING

- *To maintain relationships with friends, family, partners, work colleagues, classmates and anyone else.*

- *To have contact with people worldwide.*

- *To inform people of your whereabouts and your daily life by posting updates, tweeting or putting photographs via Instagram.*

- *To form relationships and find love.*

- *To connect with different groups and to belong to a community.*

- *To connect with classmates in school, university and college for homework and extracurricular activities.*

- *Older people connect to keep in contact and prevent social isolation.*

- *To connect with celebrities, stars, politicians, media and sports people.*

- *To connect to maintain social activities and socialising.*

- *Police use it to solve crimes and protect people.*

- *To occupy time by playing games and using other features.*

- *To use it for business purposes, blogging and vlogging.*

- *To add photographs and selfies.*

- *People use it to blog.*

- *People use it for sharing photographs of food.*

CHAPTER FIVE

The not so good effects of social media: Reasons why people don't want to connect.

"When you make a choice, you change the future."

Deepak Chopra

There are 6 billion people that have not succumbed to social networks as if it is a deadly disease that once sucked into its vacuum, there is the point of no return. As much as there are so many reasons to subscribe to Facebook, twitter and social networks, there are just as many reasons not too.

People don't want to connect as it is time consuming
For most, some find spending time on these networks can be time consuming and surprisingly boring. Depending on your circumstances, your lifestyle may be such that you simply don't have the time to allow cyber social network to consume your available time.

Some people are not logging on, simple because they can't be bothered or feel that it doesn't add any value to their lives, and rather choose treasured human moments than connections with their gadgets. People choose for it not to be a replacement for normal day to day life and creating fickle, virtual relationships with no meaning.

This is exactly what I found, that I was logging on daily and spending hours on social media, of which I later realised, I could be doing something else during that time. It was becoming time consuming and creeping up on the other aspects of my life. It became a juggling act with trying to manage family, work and then taking time out to use social media.

"Everything should be made as simple as possible, but not simpler."

Albert Einstein

Some don't connect as it is a balance of cyber relationships versus real relationships.
Yes, there is no arguing that it allows us to communicate with people around the globe, but is it a connection which should not be akinned to our normal day to day relationships of simple social interactions with people on a daily basis?

People don't want to use as it has changed the quality of our communication and relationships with others. Social network has falsely created an illusion that it has simplified our social lives and has improved our relationships. We are so immersed in this matrix and fail to realise that it is not real and our tweets, texts, status updates and pictures are all part of a virtual world. This is one of the main reasons people choose not to become loyal followers. They are the ones who are far too happy living their lives and following their dreams, than to be consumed in a virtual world.

These people prefer to have quality and meaningful relationships with those close to them. Have you ever wondered about the quality of the type of connection this offers? Gone are the days of the simple means of communication of us making a simple phone call to a friend, or sending a postcard, which were previously seemed as necessary and pleasurable.

Nowadays even making a call to a relative or loved one seems a huge task. Social media networks has created an illusion that it has simplified our lives, and therefore we continue to be loyal and in a sense trapped in this matrix, allowing for our fate to be digitalized.

"I don't use Facebook and Twitter, call me old fashioned, but I'd rather call a friend to see how they are doing. Frankly I don't have time to check their social media accounts, and why would I need to rather than call them. I don't see the point. It would be like I'm spying on them-bit too creepy for me. I think if one of my friends was going away on holiday or out, they would speak to me or call me to tell me about it. Now with Facebook and twitter anyone can see what you are doing. It might be you are out somewhere and you want your friends to know but not your boss and colleagues, so how would you be able to know who is going to see these photos."

Dr Raj -U.K

One of my closest and dearest friends and colleague psychiatrist explained how he would rather call people to know how they were doing and also to find out what was going on in their lives, rather than connecting to social media.

"I know someone whose daughter has 1000 friends on Facebook. Her family are concerned because they say she can't communicate in day to day life with people close to her. She doesn't want to be around people. She sits on Facebook and Twitter and spends all her time chatting to her so called friends. She has changed so much that she isn't the person I used to know. She doesn't even socialise when people come home."

Sonya - U.K

Not only is it changing how we communicate but also the quality of our verbal communication and social interactions. People might be popular on social media, but in real life are struggling to communicate because they are so used to using these networks. People are rather distracted by mobiles, tweets, texts and status updates when they are in company, at parties, meetings and even when going out for meals.

Wherever I go nowadays, from coffee shops like Starbucks and Costa, to Nandos, other restaurants, pubs and clubs, I see people spending their time out using social media. So many times, I have noticed people not even making eye contact and fidgeting on their mobiles. Even if they are communicating, they are using some features of their smartphones. They are constantly distracted instead of enjoying spending the time with their loved ones.

"The matrix is a world has been pulled over your eyes to blind you from the truth".

Matrix-Morpheus

And this is so true, it's created a false sense of security or grid that we are connected to people and able to communicate with anyone, anytime, anywhere. Yes, connected, but in what sense and how different is this communication compared to real life face to face contact where we are using all our senses.

When we communicate online, whether it's on Facebook or through email, or when we tweet or text, or WhatsApp, there are certain key aspects of communication that we miss. There is a unique difference in face-to-face communication and in connecting through our computer or blackberry. We end up not using all our five senses for interacting in the way it was intended to be.

It may seem obvious to some, but we tend to forget about the simple act of looking someone in the eye during a conversation. This is now becoming the norm of our daily lives. We are clearly missing the point to enjoy the moments and grasp these actual real life experiences. Now a cloud of guilt hovers over us if we don't fill family and friends in on our every move.

The digital age has vastly changed the way we communicate and it appears that we are trapped in its claws. Now, if we're on holiday in the Maldives, supposedly soaking in the sun, all we need to do is simply add an update to our Facebook status, and add a selfie photo with Instagram, or tweet our pictures and within seconds our friends and family know where we are and what we are doing.

Tap into Facebook, Twitter and Google wherever you are in the world, from a sun drenched island in the Maldives to the Virgin Atlantic flight to London, and you are guaranteed to have your finger on the pulse of what's going on in the lives of your friends, families, celebrities and politicians.

Granted with the technological age and our profile picture, this can provide us with the screen image of the person to whom we're talking. But is eye contact as palpable on a screen as it is in person, and how 'undivided' is our attention when we're reading someone's message, as opposed to when we're sitting across a table from them?

Through the smokescreen are we able to get a sense of the person who has just poked us, tweeted us or sent us a message? Can we use our senses to gauge how they look, feel, smell and how we feel around them, or get a sense of their precious smile? Surely having them close by is better than not or do we have to rely only on these sites as a means of connection.

There are certainly deficiencies in cyber relationships, as you have connected with friends, acquaintances, some people you may have known years ago, friends of friends, family, and the relationship may only exist in the cyber world.

"I communicate with some Facebook friends, but sometimes when I am in public and if I see them, some of them ignore me. I know this happens a lot with others as well. It seems so fake and I don't understand it. Why would I be good enough on Facebook but not in real life?"

Karla -South Africa

This is becoming a common occurrence. People may choose to have you as a 'facebook buddy' but then ignore you in public. In the cyber social networking there are no boundaries and limitations. Or as some people have found that their relationships in the cyber world can be relationships which actually does not materialise or cease to exist in the real world.

It's also changing the type of relationships we have. Surely there are some things we choose to tell certain people, for example, you may want to discuss your love life with your close mates and not have it on display for everyone, which includes family, work colleague and other acquaintances. It is difficult to know where to draw the line with relationships as albeit all boundaries are trespassed. This is no surprise then, as to the friction and misconceptions that these relationships are faced with.

What is the social etiquette that one should adhere to, and what are the social norms or rules. Yes, as we have gathered, they do not come with a user manual and anything and everything is possible.

Some don't connect because it causes more harm to our real life relationships.
There's no doubt that some of us may have experienced this interaction online and it has caused serious disagreements with friends and families when messages and posts are misunderstood.

"My aunt started posting stuff on Facebook that I am not a nice person and telling the rest of our family in South Africa. It's so embarrassing and hurtful. I never knew that she would be like that or especially because we were all so close and we used to babysit their kids. We don't see them anymore and miss our cousins a lot."

Surie -U.K

"I have no time for Facebook any longer. Our lives revolve around my son and hubby. I can't be bothered with all the gossip and bickering that goes on Facebook and twitter."

Dee - U.K

I have spoken to many people who have been on the receiving end of Facebook quarrels. The feuds became so unpleasant, as you can imagine, if someone posts openly about you. You cannot control who posts what and how other people interpret them.

Disagreements and quarrels are also seen now frequently amongst celebrities. It's becoming more and more prevalent the harm that people are causing with their status updates and tweets. It has caused marriages and relationships to break, some due to infidelity.

"I found out my husband was cheating on me. There were signs that he was spending more and more time on Facebook and Twitter. I then found some messages in his Facebook account and realised he was cheating on me. I didn't want to be believe it, but it's true. Facebook has destroyed mine and my children's lives. We are in the process of getting divorced."

Cara - U.K

Stories like Cara's are not surprising as Facebook has been cited in 33 percent of all divorces in the UK and social media clauses are being added to pre-nups.

CATFISH –NEV SHCULMAN'S STORY
As we know from the popular movie and series Catfish with Nev Shulman, it's easy for people to fake details about themselves. Catfish is defined as a person who creates a fake online profile in order to fraudulently seduce someone. In Nev's TV series he unveils real life stories of how people have even faked their whole lives to seduce someone. There was one episode I watched where a young lady thought she was going out with an anaesthetic student only to find out it was a young girl who just made the whole thing up. It's shocking, but it's becoming easier and easier to fake these things.

59

Writer Katie Glass in her article for Marie Claire wrote:has your relationship gone viral?

Thanks to social media, our friends can watch our make ups and break ups out in public. In her article, she explores also how everyone now has a say in your love life. She mentions also how the lift incident between Jay Z and Solange Knowles killed the fantasy of Beyoncé's relationship and how she is now reduced to people openly discussing her relationship online.

She says she judges her friend's relationships online all the time. "When I read A was back with B on facebook, my heart sank. I couldn't believe J had married E. When I spotted S tweeting B, I guessed they were shagging." You also notice when your mate's boyfriend is adding new girls or tweets when he is out clubbing on Valentine's Day. Using social media increases your family's familiarity with your loved one. With social media, it's changed the way our relationships are. It's not like just turning up to the pub with them. It's introducing them to your family, your boss, your acquaintances, your friends, even that guy you met once in a club.

Also, some people have found that words can be misinterpreted when they are isolated from body language, and posting and tagging can convey the wrong messages about how you really feel. People don't want to connect because it takes your privacy away.

Just to show the reality of this, recently a Dutch student faked a holiday to show the extent people can go through to distort the image they want to project.

ZILLA VAN DEN BORN – HER FAUX-CATION STORY
Zilla, a Dutch student, faked an entire 5 week exotic holiday to the South East from the comfort of her own home. She photo shopped herself and then posted these on facebook. She said she did this because she wanted to show just how far you can use social media to manipulate the image we want to put out to the world.

The reality is, it's all cyber related interactions and none of it is real-and that's the key difference with real relationships versus cyber relationships.
People are urged to take time to read those 5,830 words: it's Facebook that

owns the rights to do as it pleases with your data, and to sell access to it to whoever is willing to pay.

Yes, it's free to join -but with a billion of us now using it to connect, once we sign up, we lose the rights to our information. Clearly the days of you having a different image for your school, family, college, work friends or co-workers and for the other people you know are probably coming to an end quickly."

In our lives it's just not true. We can't control what happens to our information. It could be a vindictive ex-partner, or a workplace rival who may selectively expose information to your detriment.

At a recent work conference in London Thames South quay, one of the speakers informed us that the GMC or general medical council is warning professionals and doctors to behave like professionals when using social media. This is after there have been investigations and doctors have being struck off for posting details of their night out till 4 am being intoxicated and then being at work later the same day.

Even for job applications and admission to universities and colleges, employers are asking for people to disclose their social media passwords so they can be looked at before being employed. People are also having to attend work tribunals because of their social media use. And similarly a lot have been fired or victimised because of their social media use. If it seems to now already have an impact on whether we get hired or fired, I'm wondering what the future holds?

Will we never know if there's a good chance that our profiles will be used against us. The creators would like to suggest that, in an ever more transparent world, *"You have one identity"*. But as you've seen and maybe experienced, that is not true. Does anyone, know what the future holds and as to whether us subscribing to these networks is the fuel and power it needs to create a monster mesh that will eventually in some form or other will engulf us all innocent slaves and loyal followers? I guess only time will tell.

There are valid concerns of criminals
Some are urging their family and young ones to stay away from social networks because of the negative experiences they have had. Some don't want

to be victims or exposed to the more serious effects related to crime and death.

Using these networks, has resulted in valid concerns of criminals. The drawback on Facebook and twitter is that despite attempts by the police is that there are criminals lurking on Facebook and Twitter, despite privacy settings and precautions we might take, unfortunately this still puts us at risk of being their prey. Having discussed this with many people, it seems that this could be one of the main reasons which is a put off for people to consider joining Facebook and Twitter.

I personally tried to look at the various angles of this and tried to justify having a Facebook and Twitter profile knowing that I was exposing my world, my life and my family to the rest of the world allowing any criminal who has access to my profiles and details.

Some people have been prey to criminals, including sexual predators, paedophiles and stalkers. Despite privacy settings, sometimes you may post photos of children or have tagged photos of others children. How do we control who gets to view them?

We Facebookers and tweeters are possibly safe from those who are already known to the criminal justice system, however, what happens if we have subscribed to someone not knowing that they are viewing our personal and precious photos in a sexually deviant way with sexual fantasies. How on earth do we control this? Being on Facebook also may make you an easy target to be stalked.

"It feels like my life was turned upside down. I was stalked by an ex-boyfriend. He later put photos of me offering escort services. This ruined my life and I had to change all my personal details including relocating. It's so unnecessary. I am so frightened now. I have a business but I am now even scared to build a website."

Carole - U.K

It's not uncommon for admirers or fans who may start an obsessive relationship and start to stalk you or view your profile endless number of times and we would have no way of controlling this or knowing this. This is something which Carole had shared her first-hand experience of this with me. She was not only stalked and had to relocate, but this person also put a photo of her and her details, and alleged that she was a prostitute.

Evidence from research is that these social networking sites are being used widely to sexually solicit underage youth, increasing their vulnerability to sexual victimization. In addition to internet harassment, rude or mean comments and spreading of rumours.

As much as its popularity is increasing and we see Facebook and Twitter everywhere, so too are we seeing repercussions of this more and more prevalent and now even we are seeing death threats on these and other networks.

These networks are also being used to fraud vulnerable people and lure young girls.

"One of the clients I know with learning disability was financially abused by a Facebook friend. This person had requested some money and as he was vulnerable, he lent him the money. It's a bit worrying that this happen as there are so many more vulnerable people like him."

Cambridge - U.K

You lose your privacy rights

People vary with their views and some prefer to keep their lives private and they believe that exposing themselves, makes them available to the eyes of scrutiny of thousands of people and that ultimately this invades personal privacy.

Gone are those days of having some privacy and keeping what is going in your life treasured and intimate moments away from other people. Now, with simply one posting on your wall people around the globe are now privy to this information. You may have not even known that the photo that you were tagged in even existed. And no one asks permission of whether they can use your photo or not, it's just assumed that you have agreed for it to go on a blog, facebook post, tweet or Instagram.

Using social media is even more risky due to your accessible details of yourself exposed to your friends and their friends. In the virtual world of

Facebook and Twitter, there is difficulty in actually setting boundaries. This poses relationships online which may be misinterpreted by some to mean actually more than what it is.

Criminals who use Facebook would have access to some personal details as to where you live, whether you are in a relationship, have children and also, by studying your post, would be able to follow your every move. It could be that they have details of your home address and that when seeing a post of you in Paris, would realise this is the opportune time for a robbery.

Numerous deaths worldwide has been linked to the use of social network. Deaths worldwide from America, United Kingdom, India, and Mexico and virtually all over the world, have been linked due to suicide notices and threats that have been posted. Some have been affected by social networks and as a result and committed suicide.

Facebook deaths including killing of a lady by her ex-partner as she changed her status from in a relationship to single. Another lady was lured by her ex, thinking it was a reconciliation, only to be murdered by him. Love triangles resulted in stabbing and shooting in a few cases, where one even tweeted RIP after the killing.

There was a case of a 15 year old who eventually killed herself. She had on her facebook profile to 'cut and kill people' as an interest. She actually then went on to kill a 9 year old and then killed herself. Many younger kids and teenagers have committed suicide because of cyber bullying.

In October 2013 Rebecca Sedgwick committed suicide following episodes of cyberbullying.

A teenager in India, hanged herself as her parents banned her from using social network in order for her to concentrate on her studies. Also in India, there was a family dispute about land, and posts by relative, resulted in a mother of 2 hanging herself.

Neknominate is a drinking game which has also been linked to a few deaths with family of victims warning others of the potential dangers of playing this game.

As you see, as much as there are advantages, that sometimes using social networking can be deadly.

People also don't want to connect as they choose not to become a number in the virtual cemetery (Facebook and Twitter graveyards).

"I am the alpha and the omega, the first and the last."

Have you ever wondered what happens to all the profiles of people who have passed away? Having linked onto a site of someone who passed away, only 6 months later his Facebook page became a tribute and memorial for him, where people posted condolences, and thanked him for his service in the medical field and that it was a loss to society.

What's even spookier is when a person dies, however no one knows and they continue to have eternal life on Facebook and Twitter, until they find out the shocking truth via someone else, which unsurprisingly has happened. Soon Facebook, Twitter and other social network sites will be hosts of profiles of those that have deceased, and in a sense be like a 'graveyard'.

And we are back to where we started. Are these social networks becoming the alpha and the omega of our lives and those around us? Do we need to consider whether it is a means to an end, and the end to what are we making it, the end to our very existence?

REASONS PEOPLE ARE NOT CONNECTING

- *Time consuming and thus people can utilise this time for other activities.*

- *Its addictive nature as most people who use it are addicted to it.*
- *Prefer to use other forms of communication.*

- *Prefer real relationships as opposed to cyber relationships.*

- *People prefer face to face contact and quality relationships.*

- *It has been linked to causing problems between people i.e. family disputes, infidelity, disputes at home, work and school.*

- *Concerns that it's changing people's identity.*

- *People are being fired, or discriminated because of social network use.*

- *Lack of privacy.*

- *Concerns of criminals, cybercrime, paedophiles and sexual harassment.*

- *Potential to be a victim of stalking.*

- *Concerns of the effects as it has been linked to numerous deaths.*

- *Increase in the cyberbullying.*

- *It has been linked to infidelity, arguments and family feuds.*

- *People have realised that the so called friends are not actually all friends, and communicating to friends change as you communicate to a group and not an individual.*

CHAPTER SIX

The psyche behind Facebook, Twitter and other social networks.

"Without fear, we are able to see more clearly our connections to others. Without fear, we have more room for understanding and compassion. Without fear we are truly free."

Thich That Hanh

As you have been alluded to, and the more we unravel the mystery of the effects of these social networks, there are so many reasons to log on, be taken over by these networks and feel a sense of freedom of expression and a sense of being free. This has created a connection as intricate and complex as the silky threads of spider webs.

As we continue to explore these shades of blue, we get a secured sense of profiles which are attractive, soothing, and keeps us wanting more, and staying logged on and hooked in surfing and relaxing mode. Have you ever wondered why and what is the enigma of these networks that keep us logging on for more?

Communication has been made easier:
We connect because it's free, easy, simple and fast, therefore becoming the first sites to hear about the global news and thus more reliable to people who are keen to know what's going on in the world.

With all the information readily available at your fingertips, you have the birthdays of your family, friends and loved ones, and instead of sending a birthday card, wishing them on social networks, seems like the quickest and easiest way.

"Usually first thing in the morning, I would wish people for their birthdays. I know how pleased I am when I get messages from all over the globe on my birthday, and it just makes my day. It makes it easier as I am in Dubai and I have lots of friends and family in South Africa. Sending a message or tweet is instant and I know that they have got my message. I don't always get to speak to them, so knowing that I can still make a difference on their day is a blessing. I would prefer sending a card, calling or sending them a gift but that's not always possible."

Reena -Dubai

Does this sound familiar?

"My aunt passed away, and the first I heard about it was on Facebook. This saved my family time to call family around the world. I know some people were not happy about this, but at the time, we knew that it was the best way to let all our family and friends know about her death. I know we were extremely grateful that we received lots if tweets and Facebook messages of condolences from family all over the world. This support meant so much to us as a family as you know not everyone could make it for the funeral."

Anastasia -Ireland

It's become increasingly useful for people to use this as a tool to connect with families in emergencies and bereavements. It's also becoming our latest media source where we are hearing it first on these social networks. For everyday things that are going on, you can be assured that you will hear it first on these networks even before it gets to the other media.

On 12 February 2012, a twitter post revealed singer Whitney Houston's death, which was 27 minutes before it was officially announced in the media.

As you see, we can choose what we would like to do; it's free, appears to be effortless and rewarding, which is why we keep logging on. You could be anywhere, anytime of the day or night, dressed for the occasion or not, if you're in your nighties and you can connect with people. We have this amazing opportunity and gift of being able to do the unimaginable, which is to connect globally, anytime of the day, every second of every minute, 24/7 and why not take advantage and utilise this to its maximum, right? People find it easier to send friends, family, colleagues or anyone else a message as they can be assured that most will be logging into their account on a daily basis.

Socialising has been made easier
Social media has definitely affected the social network life and activity of people in various ways. With its availability on many mobile devices and smartphones, it allows users to continuously stay in touch with friends,

relatives and other acquaintances, wherever they are in the world, as long as there is access to the Internet. So what better, convenient and cost effective way is there that allows for all these purposes.

Other forms of communication you know, may take a backseat and are slowly becoming ancient. Now, instead of calling a friend or family member, it just becomes so much more convenient, free and effortless to send a message via social media.

Let us be frank here and admit that many of us, at least at one point of our lives, felt lonely. Social media has the power to be the cure for this loneliness! If you are feeling lonely, you can call a friend, go out with a group, or just spend some time with family. Instead now we prefer sending messages to our friends' Facebook or Twitter inboxes, comment on their pictures, write something fun on their walls and so on! Social media also has the power to bridge the gaps of boredom on many levels through games like candy crush, applications, music and so much more.

It also fulfils and feeds our desire, or even the need to compare ourselves to others in terms of looks, families and friends, our lives, travelled destinations, shopping, spouses and so much more. Have you ever logged on to compare yourself with one of your friends, whether it be their profile picture or checking out their latest status update or photos of their holidays?

For most, it may be that this connection is preferred to actual social contacts, because it's so much easier than living in the now and in our real lives, as it gives us a chance to escape to a place which allows us the freedom for personal expression.

Thanks to the digital age and these networks, we can enter a place where everyone speaks the same language and there's no etiquette or secret to the do's and don'ts. There's no inhibitions and fear, only the cause and effect and consequences thereafter. There's no right or wrong. We get to say what we like, what we don't like, who we would like to add as friends, and de-friend them just as quickly, and choose who we would like to tweet and what we want to tweet about.

We can escape to a place, where we feel free and we can soar to heights unimaginable. A place where we are in control of writing our life story the way we want to, whether it's fabricated or not, that doesn't matter. We are in control of who we contact, what messages we write, and we have a place to express how we feel.

"You are what you share."

Charles Leadbeater

We are looking for something outside ourselves to prove our worth and to prove that we exist and Facebook does just that. The majority of us would fit into the 'daily user' or Facebooker or tweeter, which are those who switch onto Facebook on a daily basis as if it is in our inherent biological clock to get our daily dose. The reasons for this can be few and far between as outlined below.

We connect as it gives us an opportunity to create our own domain... yourname@facebook.com or @Twitter.
For anyone who has become a Facebooker or hit the tweet button, knows that there is a force controlling you from the moment you sign that contract and there is that moment, when you hit the button of no turning back. It's like you have a relationship with this social network and in some way it becomes your companion and you are attracted to it as it becomes a means to connect with those you love, know and want to know. Others who spend up to 8 hours a day on Facebook and Twitter call it their lifeline.

The first bit of signing up is the crucial and probably the penultimate step of when you create your profile, exposing yourself to the world and in a way it's like the beginning of your life story. You initially get the opportunity to begin it and write it the way you want it to be and look like. Later on, your life story gets spiced up and then gets contributions from your friends, family and others that you choose to connect with and interact with.

Whether it is on Facebook or Twitter, Bebo or Myspace, you have to put intimate and personal details in order make your stamp into the world. The title, your domain, **yourname@facebook.com or @Twitter** no doubt appeals to you.

The sheer sound of this already has a butterfly effect of appealing to our inner psyche. In the realm and bigger scheme of things, it makes us feel somewhat important, known, recognised and having an identity, and now even a space on the internet- and why not!!

As you can see, these inventions are even working on our inner psyche (the butterfly is a symbol of our psyche: so-called butterfly effect) from the moment we agree to the thousand or so words in the agreement. It is evident that when you start using these networks, there's a force working on every bit of us and there's much more to them than meets the eye. We all need time to escape from the reality of our lives, be it exciting, boring or average, and these networks allow us to do just that.

Mark Zuckerberg has said that his Facebook profile is the core of his personality, and that's exactly what we are seeing, our personality or personalities reflected in our profiles and tweets. This is further boosted by us having to add a profile picture, and this could be anything we choose. My eldest sister Tamara shed light on one of the enigmas of social network use. She said it was so popular because people can create their alter egos and also live them through using social media as a platform.

"I think Facebook and Twitter is so popular because we can create our alter egos. People can post selfies of themselves and make themselves be something they are not. People create these alter egos to escape from the reality of their lives and make their lives look great. When people put these selfies of themselves, they want someone to like their photos and are therefore turning to cyberspace for attention, affection, love and admiration. Lots of time when people are putting those photos of themselves we don't know what goes on in the time just before and after those photos. How do we know if a couple was involved in a fight just before putting that photo of them on holiday in Greece? Or how do we know how that person was feeling at the time of taking that photo? We don't know, but people want to post these photos to create perfect images of themselves, their families,

relationships and holidays. It's in the cyber world and virtual world and it's not real."

Yes, I gathered she was right. We can create an identity to suit us and give life to our alter egos-like singer Nicki Minaj who has confessed to having as many as 15 alter egos which were created for fun, creative reasons or to escape the reality of hardships.

The cherry on the top is adding photos instantly via Instagram, which was created by Kevin Systrom and Mike Krieger, and which has the ability to boost our alter egos in the process. It's therefore not surprising its popularity that Instagram has now teamed up with Mark Zuckerberg.

The so called norm 'selfies' which is a slang term used to describe a photo that is taken of oneself for the purpose of uploading it to social networking sites, can make ourselves feel famous, cared for, glamorous, attractive and make our lives seem surreal.

Selfies are becoming now an obsession across different generations and in a sense if we continue to do so, reveals the narcissist in us. Even Kim Kardashian has put videos on how to take selfies and is in the process of completing a book on Selfies called Selfish which will have about 352 of her selfies. She was told off recently on a trip to Thailand by Kris Jenner as she aimed to take 1200 selfies in one day.

Narcissism is defined as the pursuit of gratification from vanity or egotistic admiration of one's own physical or mental attributes. As Jo Frost has warned, selfies are making children even more self-absorbed and narcissistic. The key message here is as innocent as selfies are, they can turn us into something we are not!! People from all age groups are becoming obsessed and narcissistic in taking selfies which is reaching to the stage of being addicted to it.

Recently in April 2014 after a semi-nude selfie of Rihanna was banned on twitter, she deleted her account. Kevin Systrom commented to the media that they have the right to monitor the photos and because of the concerns for the younger generation will ban nude photos.

On the other hand, we can equally make our lives seem horrible, depressing, lonely and uncared for. We can express our displeasure, voice our opinions and express our sadness in a cathartic environment, where we can get a response of support.

"In the future, everyone will be world-famous for 15 minutes."

Andy Warhol

That is exactly what we are seeing now. By creating a profile or alter ego, we get to be the star in our own story, a star on the internet landscape and we get to reinvent ourselves and alter the perceptions people have of us.

The more you peel and expose the layers, you will see no doubt that these are truly amazing inventions and therefore there it is no surprise to its popularity, effects and the power that it has over us and continues to have over us.

There's a Magnetic force of control
The magnetic force of Facebook and Twitter is in that it allowed us to connect globally throughout this world. It's a world where there is no existence of limitations and it trespasses the time differences and transcends all boundaries and cultural differences- or is it like in a sense a Utopia that we hoping to create?

"And ever has it been known that love knows not its own depth until the hour of separation."

Khalil Gibran

There is no doubt a magnetic force that is drawing us to these social media. There is a powerful force, that we realise these effects when we are not connected. We could choose to call it a connection, love, or a powerful force beyond what we can describe. Mark Zuckerburg's mother is a psychiatrist and he himself studied psychology, so there is probably more to him than meets the eye. The psyche behind Facebook and Twitter is real.

Our psyche is defined as our mind and soul. There's no doubt in my mind that there is a force that is working on our minds, whether it be consciously or subconsciously and whether or not you choose to acknowledge its existence.

We connect also because of the initial addictive effects of connecting.
Once you start logging on, and for whatever reasons, you will be aware of the trance or spell under which this technology puts its followers. It's like you succumb to an intoxicated state of wanting to keep up with the newest trends and keeping in touch with present advancements. In the same token, the withdrawal symptoms if you have not had your daily dose of logging on. I am hoping this sounds familiar as I am sure some of you have had similar experiences.

"I am at work and I spend every free moment on Facebook and twitter. I don't want to miss out on anything that's happening with my friends and family."

Andrew - U.K

It could be that from the moment you get out of bed, you check your Facebook and Twitter account and in the process your mind and body become attuned to the art of two screening and digesting information at a rapid pace. In the process your hands and fingers take on the autopilot of two screening and get accustomed to the fidgeting on the keyboards of your mobiles.

Later on, as you become an expert at social media, you could start logging on for the fear of missing out or **FOMO**, as it is now commonly known as. It has become a recognised phenomenon that it is now a word in the Oxford dictionary. It's something most users experience, where, you feel you are missing out when you are not logged on, and even when not on Facebook or Twitter, you would be wondering about a message, tweet or status update.

Recent studies have shown that FOMO is often linked to feelings of disconnection and dissatisfaction, and that social media fuels it. Think how many people constantly scan email, tweets or Facebook to keep up with friends' updates. Some people don't just want to keep up – they start to compare and evaluate their lives based on how they see others portraying their own lives.

It's clear that FOMO can affect your personal life and work life. You might have FOMO if you constantly check social media and email. This isn't about logging into Facebook a few times a day; this is feeling antsy if you can't be connected at all times. We would all like to blame our work cultures for forcing us to always be available on email, but inevitably, it's more often a choice that each individual makes. After all, we train people how to treat us and we are ultimately the ones who are in control of our use of social media and technology.

The fact is, many of us check our email and social media because we want to. We like to stay in the know, and to be on top of everything. In other words, we don't want to miss out.

We don't realize though, that we will always be missing something, but if we're spending our time worrying about it, we're missing everything.

The good news? FOMO, like most things, is a choice. When you know what's going on, you can name it and claim it. Then decide if that's really how you want to spend your precious time.

As there are no rules and no rights or wrongs for social media, the possibilities for this are endless. You would initially start spending a few minutes a day logging on or tweeting, and then maybe as the time passes and your dependence on this grows, as it would, you would start spending more and more time on social networks.

Research suggests now that the average person spends 7 hours on the internet a day, and 1-2 hours on social media spaced throughout the day. There are also many people nowadays who admit to spending every few minutes checking their accounts and some have said they use as much as 8 hours a day on social media.

This is a picture taken from Gemini Adams, author of Facebook diet.

YOU KNOW YOU'RE A FACEBOOK ADDICT WHEN

YOU CHECK-IN WHEREVER YOU GO.

FACEBOOK ADDICTION DISORDER

This is something which is real and becoming a global phenomenon whether people want to accept it or not.

An American psychologist introduced the term to describe such an addiction. FAD, or Facebook Addiction Disorder which, is a condition that is defined by hours spent on Facebook, so much time in fact that the healthy balance of the individual's life is affected. It has been said that approximately 350 million people are suffering from the disorder that is detected through a simple set of six-criteria. People who are victims of the condition must have at least 2-3 of the following criteria during a 6-8 month time period.

The criteria as you will explained later are tolerance, withdrawal symptoms, reduction of normal social and recreational activities, virtual dates, fake friends and complete addiction.

It's been described like a drug addiction to cocaine as we get a high and physical buzz because of the neurotransmitter Dopamine that's released. The pleasure producing chemical and neurotransmitter dopamine is produced in our brain every time we take in a new message or bit of information from the screen. This explains the pleasure, comfort and compulsiveness with checking our gadgets and spending hours on social networks. Each time we get a message, text, email, tweet, WhatsApp, or Facebook message, it increases our dopamine levels and it gives us that good feeling, and therefore it become like a vicious cycle that keeps us wanting to log on.

As a psychiatrist and studying the effects of neurotransmitters, I can say from my experience and knowledge that Dopamine has been linked to many mental illness, more commonly Schizophrenia and psychosis. To put it into perspective, Dopamine levels are elevated in the brain due to many illicit drugs including cannabis.

A 29-year-old woman arrives at the psychiatric clinic of the University of Athens School of medicine in Greece.

Her symptoms: mild anxiety, sleep disturbance and a loss of interest in hobbies. Instead, she spends five hours a day on Facebook. She was even fired from her job as a shop assistant because she compulsively left her post to go to an internet café.
Her diagnosis: social media addiction.

For any person with an addiction, it's difficult to acknowledge, but stories and cases of social media addiction is being commonly seen on a daily basis as people continue to be slaves to social media.

Social media addiction is the latest of internet addiction says Kristen Lindquist, professor of psychology at the University of North Carolina, Chapel Hill, because social information feels intrinsically rewarding to people. We get a jolt of dopamine when someone "likes" our Facebook post or retweets our Twitter link. Over time, the effect on the reward center in the brain is similar to what makes drug addicts go back for another line of cocaine.

"You end up developing an association between Facebook and goodness, and that sustains the behaviour," Ms Lindquist says. "As with cocaine addicts, over time you need more and more of that substance to get that feeling."

Kristen Lindquist

In another article, the writer's question was:
Is Facebook a Dopamine machine?

I guess the same could be said for Twitter and WhatsApp-Are these Dopamine machines as described above and in a sense making us the addicts we become?

We might get a great, fantastic buzz for that moment of using social media, but at the same time it's also causing **filter failure** where in those seconds of reading 50 messages, we are unable to distinguish which are important and therefore it's making us less empathic. We responding to situations in our life without emotions and feelings and in a sense we are becoming digitalised like computers.

A lot people say they turn to cyberspace and use social media when they are bored or stressed. It gives users a sense of a security blanket and staying in surfing mode, idly browsing status updates, looking at photos and reading tweets, creates a sense of relaxation.

Studies show that 60 percent of people crave stimulation and it has therefore created the multi task myth. We continue to be slaves to our gadgets because it allows us to do so much in a short space of time.

"He who learns, but does not think, is lost. He who thinks but does not learn, is in great danger."

Confucius

We are living in a time of rapidly growing social network influences. Twitter has now changed the way we learn, interact, our interests and so much more. Now, if we tap into it, anywhere in the world, we allow our fingers to be on the pulse on what's going on in the lives of our favourite celebrities, politicians, or the lives of our friends and family, in seconds. As we do, we allow them to tap into our brain or Connectome.

The human Connectome project of £35 million, are working on the brain mapping and the networks of these structures which might give us a visual insight as to how our brains actually works, the pathways, clusters, hubs and circuits of connections.

At a talk I attended in Cambridge, Professor Ed Bullmore, one of the key psychiatrists involved in this project, explained that social networks have cleverly managed to tap into our Connectome, creating a faster connection. And obviously people today are hooked onto faster connections, but at what cost. By creating faster connections, coupled with the speed of the internet, it's also making us impatient and less satisfied with normal day to day human interactions.

As you see, when you sign up to these networks, you don't realise that it is tapping into your every being. Our Connectome contributes to our intelligence and therefore it's changing the way we are learning, and training our brains to be Facebook and Twitter super brains, to read, skim, scan, surf or browse a 100 or so tweets in seconds. Honestly, how much of this are we able to register, understand, comprehend and memorise?

There's evidence to support that in this process it's making us super-fast to accomplish skimming and surfing but it's also actually weakening the neural pathways and connections in our brain. We are therefore developing brains like computers, and it's reducing our attentiveness in the process and changing our cognitive universe which is responsible for our memory.

There's further evidence to support this theory as recent studies suggest that juggling your devices like tweeting whilst watching television is directly linked to the gray matter or brain cells in our brain responsible for our memory and emotions. This recent study in Sussex shows that using these gadgets and social media could be reducing our brain cells.

PSYCHE BEHIND SOCIAL NETWORKS

• Communication

Free, easy and faster means of communication –this has allowed for us to send greetings and spread news. Connection with no boundaries and limitations. Allows us to communicate 24/7.

• Inner psyche

Allows us to create our own domain i.e. Yourdomain@facebook.com and create our mark in cyberspace and the internet. Creates our alter egos and allows us to live them in cyber space. Allows us to be a star in our own domain and live our alter egos. Allows us to belong to a community.

• Addictive effects

Releases pleasure producing dopamine which causes a buzz or high.
Taps into our Connectome or connections in our brain. Creates a sense of relaxation in surfing mode when we are stressed. Allowing us to multitask.

• Site design itself is addictive with its features

Colour blue-creates a soothing, relaxing background. Using the letter F to type facebook becomes addictive. Bulb in red with notifications and messages conditions our brains to expect this and keeps us logging on to check.
Instant notifications regarding our accounts increases temptation.

• Socializing

Creates an illusion that we are socialising but actually reduced quality of these interactions.

CHAPTER SEVEN

Which Facebook, Twitter or Selfie type are you?

"You become what you do most of the time."

Anthony Robbins

Which Facebooker, Twitter or Selfie type are you?
So once you are hooked, and you seem to be spending a lot of your free time on these social networks, this behaviour in itself can say a lot about your use.

There have been several descriptions of the various Facebooker, tweeter and Selfie types. I found these names intriguing and I am sure, that as you read this list, you will see a few of these names describes your use. Once you have read this list, you might be wondering which type you could be, and maybe you are none of them or all of them.

The importance in identifying the type you are as I did when I first laid eyes on this, is so that you can be reflective of your use social network, and maybe the next time you update you status, like a post or post a photo on Instagram, you will think about this list, and how you are being perceived?

Facebooker types

1. The "Lurker"
The Lurkers are the Peeping Toms of Facebook. These voyeurs are too cautious, or maybe too lazy, to update their status or write on your wall. You can identify them as once in a while, you'll be talking to them and they'll mention something you posted, so you know they're on your page, hiding in the shadows. The danger is that due to a lack of social contact while lurking sometimes causes loneliness or apathy among Lurkers.

2. The "Hyena"
This is the person that doesn't ever say anything, just LOLs and LMAOs at everything.

3. "Mr/Ms Popular"
This is the person that has 4500 friends for no reason. This person continues to add friends on Facebook just to show others their popularity on Facebook.

4. The "Gamer"

The Gamer plays games like candy crush with friends all day and every day. People play online games because they find it to be enjoyable and others to interact with other people from around the world.

5. The "Prophet"

The Prophet usually makes every post reference to God or Jesus.

6. The "Thief"

This person steals status updates and posts them as their own.

7. The "Cynic"

The Cynic hates their life, and everything in it, as evidenced by the sombre tone in all of their status updates. A person who believes the worst about people or the outcome of events

8. The "Collector"

This person never posts anything either, but joins every group, and becomes fans of the most random stuff. Many friend collectors send requests out of curiosity and nosiness.

9. The "Promoter"

The Promoter always sends event invitations to things that you ultimately delete or ignore.

10. The "Liker"

Never actually says anything, but always clicks the "like" button. "Liking" all of your photos, check-ins, statuses, and new friends.

11. The "Hater"

Every post revolves around someone hating on them, and they swear people are trying to ruin their life.

12. The "Anti-Proof-reader"

This person would benefit greatly from spell check, and sometimes you feel bad for them because you don't know if they were typing fast, or really can't spell.

13. The "Drama Queen/King"

This person always posts stuff like "I can't believe this!", or "They gonna make me snap today!" in the hopes that you will ask what happened, or what's wrong but then they never finish telling the story.

14. The "Womp Womp"

This person consistently tries to be funny…but never is.

15. The "News"

Always updates you on what they are doing and who they are doing it with, no matter how arbitrary.

16. The "Rooster"

Feels that it is their job to tell Facebook "Good Morning" every day.

17. The "Attention Seeker"

This is the person, usually female(you know the ones), that feel it necessary to post pictures of themselves on Facebook two to three times a day in the hopes that someone will tell them they're pretty or like the pic. Also posting selfies is the norm and slowly becoming an obsession.

18. The "Facebook Tweeter"

Those who writes statuses and comments as if they were tweets-short and abrupt.

19. The "Name Changer"

The person who always changes their name.

20. The "Insomniac"

The person who cannot sleep and wants the world to see their pain.

21. The "Facebook Moms"

The Facebook mom who usual posts include everything from the lack of sleep they are getting to where the next playgroup is. The facebook mom loves to show pictures of her little ones and may even use their faces for her profile page.

22. The "Overly Friendly Facebookers"
They collect friends like they are trading cards. They probably have never met half of their so called facebook friends. They often have interesting and/or witty facebook status posts which is why people who have only met them once keep them on their friend list.

23. The "I Love Me Facebookers"
Glamour shot did their profile picture. They also have at least one hundred pictures of themselves on their facebook page. Some of the pictures are of them which are semi-clothed.

24. The "Know It All's"
The well-meaning Facebooker who constantly updates their facebook status with the latest news and their opinions on what is going on in the world. They go on about the government and darn you if you don't agree. If you write something semi-political on your page you better believe that they will write back with their take on things, and their take is always right.

25. The "Bored Facebookers"
They fill their days filling out surveys. They take every test, pass you every bit of bling they can find, and are seemingly always on Facebook filling out yet another quiz.

26. The "Sharing Facebookers"
They love to give gifts.

27. The "Friend-Padder"
The average Facebook user has 120 friends on the site. Schmoozers and social butterflies - you know, the ones who make lifelong pals on the subway - might reasonably have 300 or 400. But sometimes have 1,000 "friends?".

28. The "Town Crier"
"Michael Jackson is dead!!!" You heard it from me first! In their rush to trumpet the news, these people also spread rumours, half-truths and innuendo.

29. The "TMIer"
Boundaries of privacy and decorum don't seem to exist for these too much-information updaters, who unabashedly offer up details about their sex lives, marital troubles and bodily functions.

30. The "Bad Grammarian"
Their posts, when you read them, you wished they had spellchecked them.

31. The "Sympathy-Baiter"
They posts reflect bad news, or attention seeking for sympathy and support from others. Genuine bad news is one thing, but these manipulative posts are just pleas for attention.

32. The "Paparazzo"
Ever visit your Facebook page and discover that someone's posted a photo of you from last weekend's party - a photo you didn't authorize and haven't even seen.

33. The "Chronic Inviter"
The person who keeps on inviting you to support their cause, play games and sign petitions.

And if you're surprised by this list then it gets better with the tweeter types.

THE TWITTER TYPES

1. The "Celebrity lover"
This is the person who loves following celebrities every move.

2. The "@star tweeter"
This is the person who follows lots of Hollywood stars or famous sports figures and tweets at them as if they are best buds.

3. The "follower obsessed or over tweeter"
Person who tweets to get followers.

4. The "FMLers"
This is the person tweeting about every bad thing that happens to them.

5. The "Noob"
This is the person whose tweets are questions.

6. The "Philosopher"
Person who tweets inspirational quotes.

7. The "incessant tweeter"
This is the person who needs to tweet all the time.

8. The "follower/unfollower"
This person first follows you, waits for you to follow back, and then unfollows you.

9. The "Blatant Self Promoters"
They are constantly talking about their business. Sure the occasional post about what they are doing business wise is fine, but these people take it to the extreme.

THE SELFIE TYPES
And if you thought the Facebook and twitter types were all that reveals your social network use, think again as the selfie revolution has taken over and continues to do so.

1. The gym selfie
It's impossible for some to go to the gym without proving it to the world and taking a quick gym mirror selfie.

2. Post gym selfie
You know this selfie, the person who is just showing off their abs or bikini figure.

3. The shy selfie
The person who is shy but as still insists on putting a selfie up.

4. The sexy selfie
The provocative looking selfie.

5. The morning selfie
The selfie you take of you in the morning, just after waking up-you know that either sleepy look or look of someone who is ready for the day.

6. The morning after selfie
 The selfie taken the night after getting lucky. The one you wished you didn't.

7. Post sex selfie
This is the one you take, to remind yourself that you getting some action.

8. The home safe selfie
Young people are being encouraged to take this selfie, the one to let everyone know that you are home safely.

9. The drunken selfie
Usually a selfie taken on a Friday or weekend from an intoxicated individual who probably won't remember sending it.

10. The under the sheets selfie
You know, the one taken from you peeping under the sheets.

11. The pet selfie
The pet lovers who want to be cute and take a photo with their pet.

12. The duck face selfie
The one taken of you trying to look like a duck face attempting to look seductive or funny.

13. The trout pout selfie
The selfie taken of a person attempting to make a trout pout face.

14. The pure poser's selfie
The people who are posing all the time in an attempt to take the perfect selfies every time.

15. The explicit selfie
These are the provocative ones. They try to pose it to look like a joke.

16. The seatbelt selfie
Some get the urge to tell people where they are driving to with this type of selfie.

17. The toilet selfie
Usually done to be funny but totally gross.

18. The holiday show off selfie
This selfie is only to incite jealousy in all recipients who are not in a sunny, posh destination.

19. The celebrity selfie
The one who posts selfies of themselves with celebrities.

20. The loved up couple selfie
Done to show how happy and perfect your love is.

21. The makeup- free selfie
Selfie with no makeup on.

22. The sick bed selfie
Selfies take at your sick bed in hospital.

23. The bikini selfie
Taken of you in a bikini.

24. The pre food selfie
Just taken before someone is about to eat.

25. The food porn selfie
The person who takes a snap of their meals.

26. The mirror selfie
The one taken of you from of a mirror reflection.

27. Getting caught sleeping selfie
The selfie taken as you get caught sleeping-maybe not one you want anyone else to see.

28. The sad selfie
The selfie taken when you want to show that you are unhappy.

29. The drinking selfie
The selfie taken to show your drinking habits.

30. The funeral selfie
The one you take at a funeral.

31. The bum selfie
The famous pose to show off your assets, like your bum.

32. The elevator selfie
The selfie taken of you in an elevator.

33. The bathroom selfie
The selfie of you taken in the bathroom.

34. The cleavage selfie
The selfie you take that clearly reveals your cleavage.

35. The jail selfie
Taken of you in jail or in police custody.

36. The getting ready selfie
The selfie taken of you getting ready.

37. The BFF selfie
The selfie taken with your best friend.

38. The 'I'm stuck in traffic' selfie
Selfie taken when you are stuck in traffic.

39. The funny face selfie
The selfie taken of what you think is funny.

40. The 'I'm having a good/bad hair day' selfie
Selfie taken of your hairdo.

41. The vacation selfie
Selfie taken of you on an exotic location- just to let everyone know what a great time you are having.

42. The 'I've just checked out my accessories' selfie
The selfie you take to show off your earrings.

43. The eye selfie
Selfie showing your eyes as the main feature.

44. The collage selfie
Selfie taken as a collage.

To be honest, a selfie can be taken anywhere, anytime, but the ones I've mentioned are the commonest ones being taken today. The gravest concern as you will read later is Selfitis and that if fuels narcissism and eating disorders.

The significance of these Facebook, Twitter and Selfie types
These types reveal to us of how our use can create us into being something which we are not or how we are being perceived. It is also true, that whatever you post or tweet, reveals some bit of your personality whether you agree or not. It might seem innocent, normal and harmless when you choose to use these networks, but your use definitely does reveal something deeper about you.

In fact, looking at all the different types of personalities, it can make us more neurotic, obsessive, narcissistic, paranoid, dependent or anxious avoidant. As Mark Zuckerberg said that his profiles reflects the core of his personality and that's exactly what our profiles are playing out in the virtual world –our personalities!

CHAPTER EIGHT

The myth of being addicted or not.

"Veni, vidi, vici. I came, I saw, I conquered and I am getting hooked."

Adapted from Julius Caesar's quote

Becoming addicted to social networks
If you are a social network user or not, there are no doubt many addictive effects of social network we need to be aware of.

There are numerous studies discussing these effects and this is something which is definitely receiving media attention and also something being researched. People are now urged to actually consider the effects be it good or not so good- so it is about **thinking before you click**.

As they tap into our every being and essence, there are unfortunately psychological ramifications of use of these social networks. Using social network allows us to connect, but as a consequence, we are not able to live in the now. We are constantly being distracted and in a sense, like Leo Babauta has said, moving from the age of information that technology has given us to an age of distraction.

"Do not dwell in the past, do not dream of the future, concentrate on the present moment."

Gautama Buddha

We are living in a now without context, without purpose, meaning...and in the process, we have made ourselves slaves to technology. There is no contesting the huge positives to our psyche that come out of technology, such as keeping in touch with friends and family all over the world via Facebook or Twitter. However useful and gratifying these connections are, it begs us to consider, are we even capable of living in the now?

So immersed are we nowadays with Tweets, texts and statuses, that even adding photos to Facebook pages or posting these on Twitter is now the norm.

If you are on vacation in the Bahamas, or at a cottage retreat, you could take selfies or photos of every detail with Instagram, and instantly let everyone, who is anyone, know about it and share in this experience. Gone are the days of sending picturesque postcards.

As convenient as it sounds, the digital age has taken over our lives, as we put the pulse of our fingers on our keyboard, above actually enjoying the moments in our lives. Yes, it might seem glamorous and great to look at later on, but how much of what we are doing are we enjoying? Our daily actions of twiddling on our gadgets are affecting our core essence of being, whether we choose to acknowledge this or not.

We have reached a state that we are not even capable of living in the now, as we forego enjoying those intimate moments in our lives and rather tweet, bbm, send status updates, using WhatsApp or spend time sexting.

Whilst capturing these special moments, of which some are essential, aren't we simply missing the point of going on holidays to rest and soak in the moments of peace, tranquillity and bliss, or going out to enjoy the tastes of our meal and relish in the company?

Are we even able to survive our treasured retreats without the added appendages we choose to use as a means of communication, survival, whose use can be akinned to the very act of breathing? I guess there are two sides to this coin for this, and for the benefits of capturing the moments, but at what cost?

As we share these special moments with people around the globe, we no doubt enter a state of bliss and pleasure, which allows us to feel that what we are doing is worth sharing and gives us that ego boost.

As we click that post of our bikini or beach body, sipping Pina Coladas on a Hawaiian beach, we get a sense we are not alone, and therefore these social networks have become our companions for wherever we are, and whatever we are doing. We are never alone and we get a secured sense that it's become our best friend.

What on earth did we do before these gadgets and social networks crept up on our existence? We only get one chance to enjoy the moments of our life, that is why, lots of professionals are using the new buzz word 'mindfulness' and teaching people the importance of living in the now, of savouring those precious moments free from distractions of our gadgets.

There's evidence now to back this up, where it's a well-known fact that people who practice mindfulness and are living in the moment, are happier people. As a consequence, to assist with this type of addiction, there are clinics that have been setup worldwide, for people to de-tech, live in the now, being mindful and meditate. Can you just imagine if you had to de-tech, de-gadget and go without your connections for a few hours a day or go for a digital detox or digital sabbatical?

Yes, it's easier said than done, as the initial symptoms of this battle are unpleasant withdrawal symptoms. When being de-teched, de-gadgeted, people started feeling edgy, less focussed, anxious, depressed, and bored, and some experience headaches; like the withdrawal of any addiction.

The thought of being disconnected and not being able to tweet, text and not being able check their statuses, are simply unbearable. There is evidence to suggest that this does not allow us to enjoy the moments, but also why people that are able to focus and concentrate on one task are happier people.

However, as those who continue to use their gadgets know, that nowadays, thanks to the digital age, just living in the present moment seems like an arduous task, where even just reading a novel without peppering it up with a tweet or text is alien.

Twoscreening on our keyboards are now as second nature, like the very act of breathing. Our traditional living rooms as you have read earlier have now been converted to a digital media hub, where we are either media meshing (using social media to communicate on related activity i.e. tweeting about the TV programme you're watching), or media stacking (using social media to communicate not related to activity). Our minds are not able to focus on one thing at a time, and we are creating a now without meaning, or we think it has a meaning.

"My biggest hobby is hanging out with my family and kids."

Joel Osteen

Gone are the days of seeing children in parks or riding out on their bicycles. Now they have an added appendage; their mobile devices, which includes mobile phones, amongst others. The musical sounds of pleasant chatter and laughter is now traded for the clicks and tweet updates.

Even when you go out now days, if you look around you, whether you are out for a meal, at the movies, gymnasium, or even at a social event like a party, how many people around you are on their phones, rather than spending time, enjoying what they are doing? People don't even communicate with each other when they are together and use their social networking to dominate their conversations.

Others might think of these social networks as a portal for leisure and fun in utilizing the various applications and games that would occupy the hours of their day. Whatever people think of it, the truth of the matter remains that Facebook and twitter, has on many different occasions, has the ability to get you hooked no doubt.

This instrument can teach, it can illuminate; yes and it can even inspire. But it can do so only to the extent that humans are determined to use it to those ends. Otherwise it is merely wires and lights in a box.

Facebook was originally started on a college campus, and we are back to where we started, and it's no doubt that the biggest impact these networks are having are with our younger generations- **Generations x and y** and soon to be **Generation alpha.**

Paediatricians, psychologists and psychiatrists are seeing an increasing amount of Facebook depression, social media dependence disorder, Facebook addiction disorder and Divided attention disorder, with people being treated in rehabilitation clinics being setup in the US, UK, Japan and worldwide. The more detrimental effects which are becoming increasingly common are cyber bullying, victimisation and harassment.

It's also making our lives two dimensional and making us think, feel and act in bytes. We call it social media and it's supposed to be for socializing, but is it. How can it be if you are at the computer alone? Real socialization involves face to face contact. The poke, smiley, hug and kisses you sent or received, isn't real is it?

"Computers are incredibly fast, accurate and stupid. Humans are incredibly slow, inaccurate and brilliant. Together they are powerful beyond imagination."

Albert Einstein

As we have seen, by choosing to connect the minutes of our day to the digital world, we are digitalizing ourselves, our mind, body and souls. We are thinking in bytes, and choosing to lose our ability to reason, and develop intuition and in the process develop a cyber-philosophy and transcendent values.

Even if we are on holiday, going out for a meal, swimming or horse riding, and by choosing to use technology, we are experimental in our experience, but we are not soaking up the experience, because we are so distracted.

By allowing ourselves to be distracted to answer emails, text, respond to our inboxes, surf social media land we are losing our ability to be productive and creative. We all need to be creative whether we are writers, schoolgoers, teachers and productive if we are working daily. How can we say that we are truly productive in our work if we are constantly distracted? Just imagine the amount of time you spend on social media and what you could have accomplished in that time. For example you could have gone to the gym, went out for a coffee with a friend, completed your household chores, done some yoga, some form of leisure like going out for a movie or just reading a book.

Our mind-set in social media, is that it's like working on a balance sheet and we do not see the richness and texture in things. It makes the moments and joys in our life two dimensional, robbing us of actually enjoying the pleasures, sounds, textures and feelings.

We are starting to see the ramifications and sequelae of overindulgence in these social networks as we continue to chase a carrot that never satisfies our appetite.

Granted social networks has made it easier for us to share our lives with those we love, and it has also helped us to reconnect with long lost school and college friends, but like all good things, it can be overdone and therefore needs to be done in moderation.

Mark Zuckerburg was quoted to saying *"I believe that learning should occur really, really young"* and we know that Facebook access is restricted to age 13 and above, despite attempts by Mark Zuckerberg to allow younger children to access this.

His sister Randi Zuckerberg who was the CEO of Facebook has recently warned parents and children about the effects of social media through her book DOT which is a story of a child hooked onto gadgets.

As you see, and whether you choose to acknowledge this or not, there's no doubt though that the bitter pill most Facebookers and Tweeters are swallowing, is the pill of addiction-and this could be the same for you.

CHAPTER NINE

The addiction explored and explained.

Ignorance is bliss

There are a number of terms being used nowadays to describe the various addictions as you will read here. I acknowledge that due to the generation differences and influences, it is difficult not to be part of social media. Having had my own personal experience of being a user of social media and seeing the evidence of the dependence people are having, I can say that the addiction is something real and something that people need to be cognisant and aware of. The good news is that if it is an addiction, then it's treatable.

I know it's difficult because some people are expected to be available all the time, carrying their mobile or a Blackberry with them, and to respond almost immediately — or they're out of touch, or are then classed as not good business people. Others are expected to be available Skype chats, or be on social networks such as Facebook or Twitter. Others need to follow the news of their industry closely, and constantly read updates of news sites.
Being connected all the time, being part of this constant stream of distraction, is an expectation that society now has of us. And going against that expectation is immensely difficult for many people — it requires courage, or a willingness to change.

How did this happen? When did we opt-in to be a part of this? There was never a time when we agreed to these expectations, but they've evolved rapidly over the last decade or so, and now it's hard to get out. I'm not saying we should get out. I'm saying we need to rethink things, to change expectations so that the system suits us, not the other way around. The initial steps would be to first identify which type of addiction it is. Below, I have explained the different types related to forms of social media.

Internet addiction disorder (IAD) was considered for the diagnostic guidelines we psychiatrists use, however, internet gaming made it to be considered a recognisable disorder. IAD is an umbrella term to include subtypes by activity, such as excessive, overwhelming, or inappropriate internet pornography use, gaming, online social networking, blogging, email, or internet shopping.

IAD is a psycho-physiological disorder characterized by tolerance; withdrawal symptoms; affective disturbances; and interruption of social relationships.

Cyber-Relationship addiction (CRA) is one impulse-control problem that is covered within Internet Addiction Disorder. A Cyber-Relationship Addiction has been described as, the addiction to social networking in all forms. Social Networking such as Facebook, Twitter, YouTube and online dating service such as uniform dating.com along with many other communication platforms. Virtual online friends start to gain more communication and importance over time to the person becoming more important than real-life family and friends.

I have mentioned in the next few pages, descriptions of the different types of conditions you get, but as explained above, these are not used for diagnostic purposes yet but merely a guide and description of what the effects of social media is having on our mental health and our wellbeing.

FACEBOOK ASSOCIATED MENTAL DISORDERS
Fear of Missing Out (FOMO)
"I am a facebook user and I check my gadgets repeatedly throughout the day. I am worried that I will be missing out in the time I am not logged on. I could be sitting at my desk, attempting to do my work, but all that's on my mind is checking my facebook account and wanting to post a tweet. It drives me crazy if I can't check my account when I want to."

Diagnosis –FOMO- Fear of missing out

Graham – U.K

FOMO is becoming more and more a reported occurrence amongst Facebook and social media users. As mentioned previously it's a now in the oxford dictionary.

It is as the acronym suggests, the fear of missing out. Users continue to have urges to log on due to the genuine fear that during the time that they are not connected, they could be missing out. As a consequence, they want to stay logged on, resulting in them spending hours logged on. In the time they are not logged on, they are spending their time thinking of it. This becomes like a vicious cycle that they become stuck in and end up logging on most of their time.

It's possible that because of this phenomenon, it results in people compulsively checking their gadgets anything from 2-20 times a day. It can become so serious that all they do is check their accounts and end up neglecting everything around them.

Facebook addiction disorder (FAD)

"I am addicted to Facebook. I cannot live without it. It's the only mean of socialising I know. I would be lost without it. I usually log on daily to check the latest updates and catch up on the latest photographs. During the day I will upload a selfie and update my status."

Diagnosis- Facebook addiction disorder

Samantha –U.K

It is described as any other addiction where a person becomes addicted and wants to log onto Facebook all the time. They slowly develop the craving, compulsion and urges to use it. As a consequence, the use of social network occupies most of their daily lives and slowly creeps up on other aspects of their lives. It could mean that they spend every free minute on using facebook. When they are not able to log on and use social network, users experience the withdrawal symptoms, like frantically craving to log on, feel anxious, miserable and a feeling of a loss of control or going crazy when they are not online.

Addiction might sound harsh to people but if you think about it, that's exactly what's happening. People are becoming more and more addicted without even realising it.

1. Tolerance

This term is used to describe the desperate behavior of a Facebook addict. They spend an increasing amount of time on the site, coming to a stage where they need it in order to obtain satisfaction or on the other extreme, it is having a detrimental effect on them as a person and their life. For the family members and friends who think they are dealing with an addict, a sign to look out for are multiple Facebook windows open. Three or more confirms that they are indeed suffering from this condition.

2. *Withdrawal symptoms*

These become obvious when one is restricted from using Facebook because they have to participate in normal everyday activities. Common signs are anxiety, distress and the need to talk about Facebook and what might have been posted on their wall in their absence.

3. *Reduction of normal social/recreational activities*

Someone suffering from FAD will reduce the time spent catching up with friends, playing sport or whatever it is they used to enjoy doing, to simply spend time on Facebook. Instead of catching up with a friend for coffee, they will send a Facebook message. A dinner date will be substituted with a messenger chat. In extreme cases, the person will even stop answering their parent's phone calls, instead insisting that they use Facebook to contact them.

4. *Virtual dates*

It is obvious that things are extreme when real dates are replaced with virtual dates. Instead of going to the movies or out to dinner, they tell their partner to be online at a certain time.

5. *Fake friends*

If 8 out of 10 people shown on their Facebook page are complete strangers, it is undeniable: they have a serious case of FAD.

6. *Complete addiction*

When they meet new people, they say their name, followed by "I'll talk to you on Facebook", or for those who are extremely bad, "I'll see you in Facebook". Their pets have Facebook pages, and any notifications, wall posts, inboxes or friend requests that they receive give them a high, one which can be compared to that gambling addicts get from the pokies or roulette table.

Facebook Dependence syndrome

"I regularly check my Facebook account. I keep in contact with my friends, family and work mates. I use it to arrange social events and keep up to date with what's going on in the lives of those close to me. I'm always available to chat online and it's how I like to spend my day. I would not be able to live without it."

Diagnosis - Facebook dependence syndrome

Emma – U.K

People that log onto social network daily appear to be mentally addicted and as a consequence can develop a dependency syndrome. For a person with this, it means that their everyday life, actions and activity will depend on social network and their lives is influenced by it on a daily basis.

It could mean that they become so addicted that they have to log onto Facebook all the time and it could then affect other aspects of their lives. This could also then mean that they end up neglecting real life relationships or they might be affected by their social network use.

People are so addicted, that they need to post everything that happens to them. When they are unable to log on, they develop withdrawal symptoms like frantically craving to log on, feel anxious, miserable and a feeling of a loss of control or going crazy when they are not online. Recent studies show that in actual fact, this type of addiction is harder to treat than any other addiction like alcohol and smoking.

Facebook Depression (FD)

There's a lot of evidence to support this-Facebook does cause depression in various ways.

"We were able to show on a moment-to-moment basis throughout the day how people's mood fluctuated depending on their Facebook usage. We measured lots and lots of other personality and behavioural dimensions, like, for example, frequency of Facebook use, but none of the factors that we assessed influenced the results. The more you used Facebook, the more your mood dropped. The negative effect of Facebook use on happiness became more pronounced the more you interacted with other people within that time frame."

Ethan Ross –researcher for Michigan University- USA

"I previously used social media in what I would now consider as an unhealthy and negative impact toward my life. I would post inappropriate things, many of which I've gotten myself in trouble for. My posts always seemed to be about any negative or pessimistic thoughts that came to my mind. The worst part was that I would post them as they came to mind without thinking about the consequences that could come from it.

I will admit that I was a social media addict, constantly checking Facebook, Twitter, and Instagram for recent posts. I would always be updating my status, posting a new picture, or tweeting something on Twitter. I would also spend hours and hours at a time on another social media blogging website *called Tumblr. Eventually, I got to the point of feeling depressed from sitting on social media sites and seeing posts about what everyone else was doing and I knew I needed to take a break. I realized I was always comparing myself and my life to others and I never thought mine was ever as good as how I had perceived everyone else's. There was always someone else who was prettier me, doing something that I wished I could be doing, or that was more popular than me. Everyone seemed to have lives that were so exciting and perfect that I began to feel as if mine was pointless."*

Carole -Texas

Psychologists and paediatricians are seeing the effects of this more and more. It is more prevalent in children and amongst teens as they obsess over the online sites. Social networks can make them feel worse especially if they feel they don't measure up and it becomes like a popularity contest. Other triggers for depression could be cyberbullying which can make the situation worse for those who are already experiencing low self-esteem. Some teens might post unkind messages which can have a psychological impact.

There are views to the idea of Facebook linked to depression. Some people feel that it could merely be a continuation of depression that children are experiencing and not a condition linked to Facebook use. However, researchers have enough evidence to show that there is a direct link that Facebook in fact does cause depression.

In severe cases, as we have seen, there has been many suicide posts, suicide attempts and people actually committing suicide as a result of the effects linked to Facebook, be it cyberbullying, sexual harassment, depression or relationship break ups.

On the one hand, the social network site, has resulted in people posting about their suicidal thoughts and plans which ended up that police, professionals, family and friends were able to intervene in time. A recent warning from a mother was that her daughter would not have killed herself had it not been for the social networking site.

TWITTER ASSOCIATED MENTAL DISORDERS
Twittourettes
This is a disorder when a person has the urges tweet and twitter. A person becomes dependent on using twitter in their daily life's and needs to tweet about everything that happens to them. Even if they are not tweeting they could be spending a lot of time reading in twitter time.

Divided attention disorder (DAD)
"Distracted from distraction by distraction."

T S Elliot

Many avid bookworms are reporting that gone are the days of simply reading a book. Their concentration span has dissolved to now to include time to pepper each chapter with a text, glance at Facebook statuses or checking their inboxes and tweets. Using social networks has created the need for us to be constantly stimulated and to multi task. Watching television whilst browsing on Facebook or tweeting, the so called two screening is second nature. We are living moments of life where we are constantly distracted and it's no wonder that it is now being called divided attention disorder.

Our brains need 6-8 seconds to respond to a story for us to react with emotion, but in twitter time, thanks to our twitter trained eyes, it is long enough for us to digest 20 to 30 tweets. Of this, how much are we able to register? In those seconds of tweeting, updating statuses, how much of this have we missed out on? Whilst we allow ourselves to be distracted, it leads to a disengaged existence as our brains are not capable of being in so many places at once.

Which means we are allowing our brains to jump from one job to another, neither completing nor concentrating. The core features of ADHD or Attention deficit hyperactive disorder or Hyperkinetic disorder are hyperactivity, inattention and impulsivity. These are similar symptoms we are seeing and in a sense a virtual form of ADHD.

As a clinician who regularly sees people with ADHD, we usually prescribe medication like Methylphenidate and Atomoxetine (Strattera-Lilly) to alleviate these symptoms. It is possible that the effects of social media could be causing a surge in these diagnosis in children and adults and in essence it might be that people with Divided Attention Disorder that are labelled as Attention Deficit Hyperactive Disorder are being prescribed medications in the future. This is the view of some of the professionals treating people with this disorder.

Twitter addiction disorder (TAD)

"I used to make jokes about my Twitter addiction, both on Twitter itself and to less 'connected' friends and relations when they made embarrassed enquiries as to what Twitter actually is. I don't any more; Twitter doesn't make me feel like laughing.

Twitter, we are told, can be as addictive as drugs. I've taken a lot of drugs. They are, indubitably, fairly moreish. Addiction was my thing. I'm a teetotaler of eight years thanks to my imbecilic propensity to excess, and since I stopped drinking and ingesting whatever stimulant I could get my hands on, the only narcotic I've allowed myself to consume is caffeine. I got married, had children and quit my youth's idiocies; what I hadn't banked on was electronic dope.

I've always liked online socialising. I started using the internet in my first job as a games journalist in 1998, and one of the first things I did when the boss's back was turned was to register for Loaded's chat room and start wasting time. This was back in the days of real-time chat' on a webpage. It felt underground. Since then we've seen the internet revolutionise the way we interact with one another, with Facebook emerging as the global connectivity poster boy, but nothing else matches the pure buzz of Twitter. I use Twitter constantly, all day, from the moment I wake up to the last minutes before I go to sleep. It's not unusual for me to check Twitter on my phone before I turn on the light in the morning, and I usually do a few last refreshes after my wife plunges our bedroom into darkness at night. I have a Twitter app open on at least three devices in the house at any one time: on my PC in my office, on a laptop in the kitchen, on my smartphone or on my Vita. I use Twitter during meals, before I start my car's engine, when we go for family walks and when I travel on trains. I don't read when I sit down to 'relax': I tweet."

If Facebook's the mainstream social gateway, Twitter's the hard stuff. Everything about it provides instant, constant gratification. Nothing epitomises 'f5 syndrome' - the desire to repeatedly refresh a webpage or app - better than Twitter. The 140 character limit on tweets means it takes seconds to contribute or notify, and the codification of posts, with their insignia for replies, direct messages and hashtags, gives a seductive, cliquey impression. When you stand on the outside and watch people voraciously using something, the urge is to join. Once you've on the inside of a universally addicted group, leaving can be very difficult.

Simon - U.K

Twitter addiction is described as any other addiction where a person becomes addicted and wants to Tweet or stay logged onto it all the time. They slowly develop the craving, compulsion and urges to tweet. As a consequence, the use of twitter occupies most of their daily lives and slowly creeps up on other aspects of their lives. When they are not able to tweet and use social network users experience withdrawal symptoms as mentioned previously.

Social network dependence syndrome
This is a dependence and addiction to social networks. Be it Twitter, Facebook, Myspace, Bebo, Pint interest, Instagram or YouTube, where people are logging on whether it is every day, minute, hour and this is causing them to be dependent on social networks so much so that it can be compared to the act of breathing, that if not connected, it feels as if their life support is taken away.

This dependence could transgress into various aspects of their life affecting their relationships with family, their social, and work life too.

WhatsAppatitis (WHAT)
This is known as a disorder of the injuries to joints related to overuse of social messaging WhatsApp. The first person to have been diagnosed with it, presented to pains in both her wrists. According to Orthopaedic surgeons in India, the cause of this is the way a person uses the touch screen with either palm facing the device on either side or the thumbs flying at the screen. They have seen a lot of cases with people presenting with this type of pain. Furthermore it can also affect the ulnar ligaments of the hand and other joints.

WhatsAppatitis also falls into a known category of disorders called Repetitive Stress Injury due to repetitive use of devices. Other disorders associated with it are carpal tunnel syndrome.

Suicide messages
As we have seen earlier, the more serious effects which have been seen are when social media is being used as a platform for suicide announcements.

The media and the internet may be having an influence on suicidal behaviour. According to the research there are numerous reports of suicide notes on Facebook, Twitter and recently as I recently saw a case on WhatsApp. There have been people who have gone to the extent of the Copycat suicide which is called the Werther Effect.

It is still unclear as to the overall effect of such notes which will in fact lead to greater encouragement of suicide, prevention or to greater opportunities for suicide. The successful suicides following suicide notes on Facebook has occurred in various countries, America, Spain and Scotland where the people committed suicide within hours of their suicide notes.

Eating disorders
There is now clear evidence that the use of social media affects a person's existing eating disorder and can also cause them through various avenues explained below.

"I work with college students every day in my job overseeing the National Eating Disorders youth outreach. For those who struggle with poor body image, perfectionism or anxiety - just a few of the many risk factors associated with disordered eating - social media can be downright toxic.

Facebook, Instagram, Tumblr, Twitter, Pinterest and their many others do provide an unprecedented degree of access to images and messages that can entrench and sometimes trigger disordered eating thoughts and behaviors. Frequent users of social media can end up feeling as though they're alternating between broadcast and comparison modes, which are both dangerous places to be if you are prone to believing that your self-worth is based on others' approval."

Anna – U.K

Food porn

This is so common and now a norm. Be it at a restaurant or a meal you cooked, and hey presto with Instagram at your fingertips you can share this with anyone.

Food porn is by definition known as the glamourized spectacular visual presentation of cooking and eating. The foods displayed usually boast a high fat and calorie content and some exotics dishes arouse the desire to eat, and seen as a substitute for sex. Every time someone is cooking, or going out, they have the desire to take an Instagram photo and share it with everyone. As innocent as this act may be, in actual fact it's fuelling into eating disorders.

According to researchers, people spend a lot of time on this as it makes them feel good, and as it's so addictive, they can spend any amount of time on it. Later on, it can become an obsession.

A growing evidence into this suggests that this actually feeds into a person's eating disorder and causing an emerging epidemic of eating disorders.
Dr Oz has suggested that looking at food porn makes you fat. And he is right as groups of people who suffer from eating disorders like anorexia, bulimia and obesity are blaming social network use.

Selfies

A Selfie is as a picture taken of yourself with a smartphone or webcam that is planned to be uploaded to Facebook, Twitter, Myspace or any other social networking site. It usually starts with a certain angle with a smartphone tilted at 45 degrees, with a good light source.

According to a recent study in the international journal of eating disorders, regular Facebook, Twitter and Instagram sharing in young women has been found to be directly associated with an increased risk of developing an eating disorder.

"When I look at other people's albums on Facebook, the comparing is automatic. I end up feeling like crap." I used to stare at my thighs in the mirror, wishing they could be as thin as those of models in the pictures I tore out of magazines. Nowadays, hashtags like #thighgap, which have turned appearance-related fixations into searchable universes with never

ending streams of photos and "thinspirational" text. I wanted desperately to be liked waiting for "likes" or "hearts". The point is that the obsessions, compulsions and comparisons that drive eating disorders are nothing new. Social media has just amplified them.

Some might choose to unplug from social media to protect their mental health; there's a reason that most residential eating disorder treatment centers ban social media use among patients. But the reality is that most people at risk or actively struggling with disordered eating use social media in some way."

Tasha –U.K

Selfies are constantly being manipulated and angled so that the subject of the photo can appear more attractive than they may actually think they are. This practice alone encourages a culture of dissatisfaction with one's natural body image. Young girls and women view these photos of their friends and start to believe that's how they are supposed to look which then feeds into their eating disorder.

This act of taking selfies is becoming an obsession and people are becoming more narcissist or self-absorbed. Something which will probably become recognised but not a recognisable disorder is selfitis, which is the obsession of taking selfies. Taking selfies revolution is taking the world by storm and people are becoming uncontrollable. Where does the beginning of normality start and where does it end for a selfie doer. Is taking up to 200-1200 selfies a day normal behaviour. If you're a selfie doer, can you say without certainty that your taking selfies is not an obsession and not feeding into your vanity, looks, desires, mental health and wellbeing?

Applause hunger
How many times have you uploaded a photo, waiting for the likes to stream in? This is actually as applause hunger, where there is a constant need for applause and validation of people's Instagram, profile pics and selfies.
According to a psychologist, there is a concern by parents that this new and risky practice could spread like wildfire and develop a new wave epidemic in teen eating disorder. As a result of this new phenomena of people putting photos of themselves for likes, thumbs up and hearts they can accumulate,

they rely on the public to boost their self-esteem. And on the flipside if they do not get enough likes then it could mean that this can cause affect their self-esteem negatively.

Other effects of social media related to mental disorders

According to a well-known psychiatrist Dr David Veale, United Kingdom, he is seeing more and more cases of people obsessed with taking selfies and this is linked to **Body Dysmorphic Disorder**. Sufferers usually are concerned that they have a physical defect and seek constant reassurance, whilst repeatedly checking in the mirror or now taking selfies in different angles that do not show any defects or flaws.

"Dannie was a teenager who tried to kill himself after falling into a downward spiral of depression characterised by Body dysmorphic disorder and compulsive selfie taking.

He said-It becomes a mission to get approval and it can destroy anyone. He would pose up to 200 selfies per day. It's a real problem like drugs, alcohol and gambling. I don't want anyone to go through what I've been through."

Dannie Bowman – U.K

Dr Veale treated him and emphasised that cases like Dannie's was not about vanity but about technology and social trends enabling individual's latent mental problems. As a consequence of this, surgeons are seeing more and more people for reconstructive surgery to correct these flaws. So thousands of pounds and dollars later we see people undergoing the knife in an attempt to create the perfect selfie. This seems extreme but it is becoming a reality as it now affects even younger people who are willing to undergo the knife to perfect their appearances.

Sleep disturbances due to reversal of sleep wake cycle

There could be various reasons for logging on in the early hours of the morning, however, it does cause sleep deprivation and disturbance. Many users are using social media the first thing in the morning or the last thing when they go to bed.

Sleep disturbance in itself can have other repercussions and manifest in other ways, impacting on our general psyche. Here we are seeing a reversal of the sleep wake cycle, where a person is sleeping in the day, and spending most of the night and early hours of the morning on Facebook or Twitter.

The net effect is that we are seeing that more and more night is turning into day for teenagers and adolescents, despite the fact that we humans are built to sleep at night. Less sleep will mean more weight, more fatigue, and lower mood, as people don't give their bodies a chance to rebuild. Rest is regeneration – and that is how your body stays healthy and alive. Social networking is now viewed by large parts of the population as an integral part of life so important they will engage it all day and through the night which is the prediction for the **Generation z** – born from 2010 and **Generation alpha**.

Causing an impact on our emotional psyche

Some people find that posting their everyday experiences are a good thing to do. Others use it at their leisure. Irrespective of what reasons you use to post something on your wall the psyche behind that is that it is something you want to share with 'your close friends, family and colleagues' .

The hope is that this will cause some reaction to you and to others. However it can also be that no one responds or the response might not be what you envisaged, and that can also affect you emotionally. In the cyber world there is no boundaries and limitations and therefore some people have no hesitation in sharing some intimate details and inappropriate comments, which in a normal social interaction would be taboo.

I think the main drawback of this is that you cannot control what gets posted on your wall or not. So how do you get rid of that 'childish post' someone posted, which you clearly do not see as amusing.

Also people post of people who they feel at that time, and moment they need to. This can cause some discomfort and uneasiness in the cyber world of communication where someone close to you might be wondering, but why he didn't or she post something on my wall or hasn't answered my message.

Affecting people with underlying mental illness

Other addictions we need to be mindful are that people with mental illness are also using these networks, and I have seen lots of cases where a person with Schizophrenia has updated his status and added photos suggesting that he was becoming more paranoid and had some strange beliefs about time travel and the machine he created for this. Similarly, people with bipolar affective disorder could be having a manic episode and thus could be sending a lot of messages, making impulsive decisions, become more promiscuous and spend little time sleeping.

It works both ways I think. Social media has shown to have a positive effect of being a support network for people with mental illness, but on the other hand, it can trigger a relapse if people are spending a lot of time, becoming addicted and as a consequence not taking care of their mental health and wellbeing. It can also trigger a relapse for those if there are increased stressors; like due to arguments, cyberbullying, misperception and miscommunication.

Other addictions for the future
IPad addiction, YouTube addiction, insta addiction and i-disorder are other terms which will soon become a reality for those who continue to use these types of devices and media.

Summary of the different type of addictions
Cyber related addiction
The mental disorders associated with social network use
Facebook
- *Fear of missing out (FOMO)*
- *Facebook addiction disorder (FAD)*
- *Facebook dependence syndrome*
- *Facebook Depression*

Twitter
- *Fear of missing out (FOMO)*
- *Twittourettes disorder*
- *Twitter Addiction disorder*
- *Divided attention disorder (DAD)*

Social network
- *Social network dependence syndrome*

WhatsApp
- *Whatsappatitis (WHAT)*

Social media suicide messages include use of Facebook, Twitter and WhatsApp.

Eating disorders: Anorexia nervosa and Bulimia nervosa, Body Dysmorphic disorders.
Selfitis
Other
- *Related to mental disorders like Depression, Schizophrenia, OCD (obsessive compulsive disorder), Anxiety and Bipolar Affective disorder), Autism, Panic disorder*
- *Sleep Disturbances*

Disorder	Symptoms	Signs
FOMO (Fear of missing out)	• Logging onto Facebook or twitter because you might have missed out. • If you are not logged on you believe that you might be missing out.	• Logging on daily and more than 4 times a day to catch up on tweets and status updates. • In severe cases staying logged on. • Checking your devices every free moment you have. • Later on onset of anxiety symptoms.
Facebook addiction disorder	• Addicted to using Facebook. • Using it for more than 1 hour per day. • Starting to affect daily life, work relationships, school, business. • Using facebook when bored or stressed. • Updating status, taking selfies and adding photos. • Desire to let people know your every move.	• Intense craving. • Strong urges to use. • Compulsion to use. • Compulsive and repeatedly checking gadgets. • Tolerance develops. • Withdrawal symptoms- anxiety, jittery, feeling miserable, losing control and going crazy.
Facebook dependence syndrome	• Dependent on Facebook for everyday life-i.e. relationships, work, school, college, business.	• Living in virtual world more than in reality. • Prefers this type of contact. • Everyday life dependent on social.

Disorder	Symptom	Signs
Facebook depression Additional triggers cyberbullying, relationship problems	• Feeling unhappy or sad for more than 2 weeks. • Experiencing low self-esteem. • Decreased confidence. • Feeling that you don't match up to others. • Feeling of jealousy.	• Decreased/increased appetite. • Decreased/increased weight. • Decreased or increased sleep. • Unable to enjoy hobbies. • Decreased energy. • Decreased motivation. • Severe cases feeling suicidal or that life is not worth living.
Twitter addiction disorder	• Addicted to using twitter. • Prefers surfing in twitter time than engaging in conversations.	• Logging on daily and more than 4 times a day to catch up on tweets and status updates. • In severe cases staying logged on. • Checking your devices every free moment you have.
Twittourettes	• Addicted to tweeting and reading tweets. • Repeated checking of gadgets.	• Sending tweets daily. • Updating tweets with photos taken by Instagram. • Spending more than an hour reading tweets.

Disorder	Symptoms	Signs
Divided attention disorder (DAD)	• **Distracted by social network use.**	• **Distracted by use of gadgets.** • **Inattentive and have difficulty focussing attention.** • **Impulsive decisions and impulsive use of social network.** • **Becoming hyperactive because of social network use.** • **Multi-tasking.** • **Jumping from one task to the next without completing.**
Social network dependence syndrome	• **Dependent to social networks.** • **Intense desire to use social networks.**	• **Dependent to social networks.** • **Intense craving.** • **Intense compulsion.** • **Increasing tolerance.** • **Withdrawal symptoms.** • **Neglect of other pursuits.**
Whatsappatitis(WHAT)	• **Injury to joints of hands and wrists.** • **Constantly using WhatsApp during the day.**	• **Pain in joints.** • **Swelling and redness.** • **Ulnar joint problems and carpal tunnel syndrome.**

Disorder	Symptoms	Signs
Eating disorders 1. Anorexia Nervosa. 2. Bulimia Nervosa. 3. Obesity. 4. Body dysmorphic disorder. 5. Triggered by food porn, applause hunger, selfies, selfitis and peer pressure.	• Related to triggering a relapse or causing these disorders	• Same as for each disorder.
Mental disorders	• Affects mental disorders like Schizophrenia, Psychosis, Bipolar affective disorder, Depression, Anxiety, Obsessive compulsive disorder, Autism, Social Phobias, Personality disorders and drug and alcohol addiction.	• Same signs as in each disorder.
Future disorders 1. IPad addiction 2. YouTube addiction 3 i-disorder 4 Insta addiction	• Addiction to using iPad. • Addiction to YouTube. • Addiction to i-devices. Addiction to Instagram	• Similar to other addictions

Disorders	Symptoms	Signs
Sleep disturbance	• Reversal of sleep wake cycle. • Insomnia in severe cases.	• Decreased need for sleep. • Using social network throughout early hours of the morning • Tired or fatigue during the day. • Weight gain.
Emotional effects	• Awaiting for an immediate response. • Worrying about Facebook and tweets. • Sharing problems online. • Causing arguments and disagreements. • Decline in work and academic performance.	• Feeling stressed. • Intense worry. • Increase anxiety. • Victim of cyberbullying. • Feeling depressed. • Decreased self-esteem. • Decreased confidence. • Poor memory and concentration.
Cyber crime	• Victim of cybercrime because of social media use. • Due to stalking. • Due to burglary. • Due to fraud. • Due to sexual assault. • Due to profiles exposed to criminals and paedophiles. • Due to being vulnerable.	• Signs related to each crime.

CHAPTER TEN

The warning signs - Can't do with it, can't do without it.

How do you know if you are in trouble and need to get help with your social network use?

I guess we as individuals owe it to ourselves, our family, friends and work to **think before we click.** As you have seen, whether we have chosen to acknowledge the impact of social network or not, it is crystal clear it is having an impact!

For those readers who are willing to face this, then there are the initial tell-tale signs that Facebook, Twitter, and other networks are beginning to have an impact on your everyday psyche. The onset of this could present with the following features related to your use of social media:

CHECKLIST FOR WARNING SIGNS THAT YOU ARE BECOMING ADDICTED TO SOCIAL NETWORKS

1. You use social media to help you with your problems in real life. You could experience a sense of loneliness, isolation and feeling of being sad or depressed when not online. In more extreme cases, this could even go to the extent of putting suicide and threat messages. √/x

2. As a consequence of spending hours on social networks, you neglect taking care of yourself, including eating healthy, exercising and having adequate sleep. √/x

3. This could also because you to delay completing tasks, homework and miss appointments. It can cause a decline in your grades, overall academic and work performance. √/x

4. You may also neglect your other pursuits, family, friends, work and hobbies. √/x

5. Facebook, Twitter, Myspace and Bebo, amongst others becomes a replacement for close relationships, and you realise you are conducting your relationships with these networks, and this slowly causes your real time relationships and face to face contact to fade away. √/x

6. You could start to have conflict at work or at school because of your social network activity. You end up lying about your time on social media.

7. You could experience the repercussions of your social media use and be taken to a work tribunal because of it. √/x

8. You begin to experience the physical effects because of being overstimulated and lack of sleep. You could begin to feel tired, irritable, and slowly signs of depression creep in. You could experience weight changes (loss or gain), stiffness, anxiety and carpal tunnel syndrome. √/x

9. You could start to experience the psychological effects of cyber-bullying and harassment. √/x

10. You begin to realise that the more you log on and choose to click, you become hooked and dependent on these networks, and it becomes a part of your daily routine. √/x

11. When you are not able to log on, you experience a genuine fear of missing out (FOMO). √/x

Score /11

CHAPTER ELEVEN

Living in the now to survive
Facebook and Twitter addictions.

"Be happy in the moment, that's enough. Each moment is all you need, not more. Live in the now, enjoy the moments, savour the sounds, smells, tastes, touch and enjoy the company you are with."

Mother Teresa

"Live your life consciously."

Steve Pavlina

So if you're reading this, you are wondering, how you strike a balance to survive social networks, knowing the good, not so good and glamorous effects it has on our lives. Some of you reading this might even think that there is no issue with being on these networks, and therefore continue to choose to live your existence, by logging on.

For those, however who think, that maybe, there are some effects as a consequence, the message is clear- *think before you click and live in the now.*

"We want to convince ourselves we are in control."

Jodie Picoult

'I love you'- is the inscription inside Pandora's Box.

So how do you keep your sanity when social networking has you compulsively logging on every second or minute, to check your updates? You know you are spending every free moment checking on your account, ensuring that you have not missed out on the experiences in the day, aka; FOMO.

How do you strike a balance in being connected and still managing your day to day life? As a parent you might be wondering what on earth your 16 year old is posting on their wall, and as no surprise, you are not privy to being on their wall. Sometimes, in desperation, you might even be thinking of spying on your child. These are the typical everyday dilemmas people are faced with, and probably why some of those wiser ones are not subscribed.

Having peeled the intricate layers of these networks and seen the good, not so good, and the glamorous effects, like with all good things in life, and that it's about striking a balance and about moderation. We know we should eat chocolates in moderation or should drink in moderation, and that any excess could have some effects on our physical and mental health and that's not rocket science, and therefore the same golden principles apply.

When you sign up to Facebook, Twitter, Myspace, Bebo, YouTube etc. you have a choice and you know that you are going to write the story of your life. What springs to mind and looking at Obamas warnings that things from your younger days will come to haunt you.

Reader, if you choose to be on Facebook or twitter, and each time you log on, and feel that sensational buzz, think twice, and think that if you were 5 years, 10 years, 20 or 30 years down the line, would you be happy with the life story you have written. Are you happy with the posts, messages, tweets, photos? How are you going to feel if your future spouse, children and colleagues are going to see those posts?

There's no arguing that it is exciting and amazing, that we have the opportunities to do these amazing things, we could never have dreamed of, and yes there are so many positives as it boosts to our life. So much so that now we feel that we cannot live without these connections as if, it's part of our breathing and that if taken away, it would be taking away our life support. Sounds extreme, but this is a harsh reality some people are facing as they continue to live in the battlefield of social media effects instead of having tweet and facebook freedom.

CHAPTER TWELVE

*Social network detox diet -
working towards wellbeing and
recovery.*

"Be the change you want to see in the world."

Mahatma Gandhi

"Most of what we say and do is not essential. If you can eliminate it, you'll have more time, and more tranquillity. Ask yourself at every moment, 'Is this necessary?"

Marcus Aurelius

STEP ONE
To de-tech or not to de-tech, that is the question?

Making a positive change and de-tech into the future
For any addiction, abstinence is obviously the best solution. It's obviously easier said than done. There have been many success stories of people who have made a change of either stopping it altogether or making a change towards tackling their social media use.

I am not saying that you need to give up social media completely, but I am asking you to consider the effects that social media has on you or your family or loved one. If you think that there could be a problem then I want you to consider whether you need to stop using social networks or control the amount of time that you do spend on it in order to be a happier person, who is productive and fulfilling their goals.

Steve Pavlina is a world renowned author on self-growth. In his personal journey to tackle his use of social media and checking emails in November 2013, he limited himself to checking this 3 times a week.

During his experiment, he found that he was able to focus on his goals and projects, get more done and thus be more productive. He started to notice a drop in how important social media was and lost a desire to post for the sake of posting. He was also able to avoid late night communication and go to bed at a consistent time.

The bonus for him was that he started to notice the abundance of time he had, and thus was able to incorporate time to exercise. The mental and emotional itch to do frequent checks to at random times faded significantly.

He noticed that he became less aware of online friends and more aware of people close to him. He was enjoying the time he spent with his kids and felt more engaged.

And more surprisingly recently on 7ᵗʰ July 2014 he posted on his website, 'social media you got dumped' and closed his Twitter, Google, Facebook and YouTube accounts. I read his entry with amazement as he explained the reasons for doing this, as he previously tried to do this in 2011 but returned to using social media.

It was like reading that someone else out there, feels exactly how I do about the effects of social media, and that he was brave enough to close all his accounts. A lot of what he has written about makes perfect sense and is in sense similar to my predictions.

Coincidentally, Steve's mantra is to live life consciously and it's not surprising that this is way forward, to live our lives consciously and become aware of every moment than by being distracted by social media.

There's more to focus and beating distraction than just creating. Constant connectivity and distractions, and a lack of focus, can affect our peace of mind, our stress levels, and our happiness. I am sure that every person on this earth wants to lead a happy life or it's what we all strive for. And it can be yours, but you need to consider your relationship with your gadgets. I'm in no way saying that you should not use technology, as I know that it benefits us all, but we need to consider when enough is enough, like in Arielle Ford's case.

Author of Wasabi love , Arielle Ford wrote, 'my addiction: rings, dings and pings", in June 2013 and explained how due to the amount of rings, dings and pings, coming from emails, texts, and Facebook IMs in just 60 seconds, she realised that it must not be good for her nervous system and longed for a tech detox. Later on in October 2013, due to this and other reasons, she de-teched and is learning to reboot, rethink, rest and rejuvenate.

MY STORY

"I don't check my facebook or twitter account as I did previously. Neither do I turn my computer on in the morning. My morning is spent just enjoying a cup of tea or coffee. I take time to write, do yoga, meditate or go for a jog. I know I am not missing out on anything.

It's a wonderful feeling of being facebook and twitter free. I soak and enjoy the quietness of the morning and my day. Whilst I am disconnected from technology and social media, I am strengthening my connection with life, enjoy the beauty of nature and the people around me. I make time to meet friends, family and go on different outings with my little ones, whether it's for a Costa or Starbucks hot chocolate, going for a walk to the lake to feed the ducks, making ceramics, or just going to the park.....I am loving every minute and it feels so good-that I wished every person could have this glorious feeling of disconnection. My life is filled with unbeatable, amazing and magical moments that I could not trade for with on screen relationships."

Social media has given us so much, empowered us and we do need it. But I'm a firm believer that there's always a time and place for it and that's where each person would need to strike a balance.

I guess in the world we live today and having knowledge of the different generations we have to go with the times and use our gadgets for social media. That's fine and as we have seen there are huge positives that come out of this. However, when it starts to have an impact on our lives and health and on the people around us whom we care about, then we need to consider whether this is good or not and whether we need to do something about our use.

There are *so many benefits of disconnecting* and I have listed only a few below:
*Being disconnected allows you being to live your life consciously, free from distractions, and therefore you will be able to focus better.
*You will find that you have more time to be creative and to work.
*You will be able to connect with real people, those that matter to you and socialise in real world as opposed to the cyber world.
*You can work towards your goals and accomplish more and maybe do those things that you have meant to complete like climb a mountain, learn a new

dance, complete a cooking course or learn a new language.

*You get to relax and get away from the stress of being distracted and stimulated-because let's admit it, using our gadgets can be stressful and tiring especially if we have to keep up with what's going on

*You can start develop a peace of mind.

*You can start to be happy in living in the present moment and enjoy all the rich experiences without having to turn to cyber world.

*You will get more time for solitude. As a psychiatrist, we learn that quiet, solitude and reflection leads to greater happiness when they're a part of our daily lives. What you do during this time — read, write, run, nap, sit, watch, listen, even have a quiet conversation, play, study or build something.

Working towards Social network detox

If you decide to disconnect completely from your social network use all together, all you need to do is log onto your account and deactivate your account. However, if it's not that easy for you, read on further on how to de-tech or go on a digital sabbatical or facebook/twitter and social network diet.

STEPS TO DELETE ACCOUNT
- *Log onto your facebook, Twitter, Google or YouTube account.*
- *If you're serious-you can make an announcement on your profiles that you will be closing your accounts.*
- *Go to settings.*
- *Deactivate accounts.*
- *Delete account.*

STEP TWO
If you are feeling motivated, and you feel you need to do something, my best advice would be to start with using the **HEART (Happily ever active recovery tool) for social media detox which I have included in this book as an aid memoire,** to monitor and tackle your social media use. Ideally this should be done for 30 days to assess the progress you have made.

This tool is for anyone who wants to reduce the amount of time that they are spending on social networks. It could be that you are someone who wants to pursue their goals, improve your grades, improve the quality of your real life relationships or just be more productive and creative.

Begin by treating your use of social media like a relationship.
Social media is something that we are using to conduct our relationships and therefore it needs to be treated as such. This is exactly what Dr Nerina Ramlakhan, author of Tired but Wired: How To Overcome Your Sleep Problems, explains in her book.

Identify the triggers that lead you to use social network
In order to overcome the dependence or addiction that you have, you need to think about the relationship you have with social network. Some ways of looking at it, is to identify what are your triggers to using social network

Identify the trigger
For example, why do you look at facebook or twitter first thing in the morning? Is it because you are bored or lonely? Or do you use it when you are feeling stressed?
*Once you have identified that, **find a new positive habit to replace** the old habit for each trigger.*
For example, instead of looking at it first thing in the morning, take out time to enjoy a cup of tea or coffee, do some meditation or write or spend time with your loved ones-gadget free and maybe listen to some music.
If you doing it because you are stressed, learning relaxation techniques or listen to relaxing music.
*In order to ensure that you will continue to perform the new habit as opposed to the old habit, you need **to create a positive feedback** for the new habit. If it's not enjoyable you will quit. Getting praise from others is also a great way for receiving good positive feedback.*
*Equally important is creating an **instant negative feedback** for the old habit. Make it a rule that you have to call someone and tell them if you have failed when you go online.*

As it is an addiction with urges, you need to realise that it's only temporary. If you are having an urge, you can flow with it, it will surge, get stronger and then fade away. Take some deep breaths and then replace the habit with another one. Once you have identified the triggers and listed them, then start to monitor your use with the HEART recovery tool as I have explained later on.

Here's an example of a trigger list and list to replace the old habit which you could write out:

My List of triggers for social media use:
I log onto facebook when I am bored.
I log onto facebook first thing in the morning.
I log onto facebook or twitter when I am stressed.

I am replacing my habit of using social media with:
Meditating.
Having my morning coffee/tea/breakfast gadget free.
Spending time with my love ones.
Listening to music.

Once you have identified your triggers, then you could start to monitor your use of social media with the HEART (Happily ever active recovery tool for social media detox/diet)

Sample of HEART for Social media detox/diet
Happily ever active recovery tool for social media detox/diet

Social network CBT ©

Sample

Weekday	Time on social media	No of times checking gadgets or having itch to do	Time for activities Exercise, leisure, Calling someone	Effect on mood Sleep energy levels	Long term goals	Withdrawal Symptoms- Craving, compulsion, Checking, anxiety, jittery, losing control ,FOMO
Monday	Am Pm Evening					
Tuesday	Am Pm Evening					
Wednesday	Am Pm Evening					
Thursday	Am Pm Evening					
Friday	Am Pm Evening					
Saturday	Am Pm Evening					
Sunday	Am Pm Evening					

Happily ever active recovery tool (HEART) for Social media detox/diet explained

This is the explanation for the simple tool that you will need to use to overcome this social network addiction or dependence you might be experiencing. To make maximum use of this, try to incorporate all of these in tracking and monitoring your social network use. I have included at the end of this chapter a 30 day plan, which you can use to get started and on track. It's a quick and easy way to monitor your social media use and you can use 30 seconds to 30 minutes to complete it. Once you have completed it, you will be able to reflect on your social media use and see your progress or areas that need further improvement.

Reducing your social media use is achievable and there are many people who have successfully stopped or who are going on digital sabbatical, so it's worth you attempting. I know it's easier said than done, but just think about the benefits of even just attempting it, then you have won half the battle...and a step closer to a happyish you, living and enjoying every moment of your life that matters in the real world as opposed to the digital world. Trust me, anyone can do this and you can too....

Step 1
Tracking and monitoring your time spent on social media
Monitor the amount of time you spend on social media and also document the number of times you check your gadgets during the day. Once you have identified this, then consider developing rituals as explained later. Ensure that you incorporate time for other activities. Also try to monitor the effect of social media use on your mood, sleeping habits and any withdrawal symptoms.

• Develop focus rituals or routines to reduce the amount of time spent on social media
In order to be successful in tackling this dependence, developing rituals will help keep you on the road to success. We all have rituals which we probably don't realise, but they work because they are a set of actions that we perform habitually. As discussed earlier we need to replace the habit or addiction of using social media with other rituals.

Some suggestions by author Leo Babauta are to develop the following rituals:

*morning quiet- develop a morning quiet ritual when you start your day before the busy-ness of the world intrudes on your peace of mind. The key to enjoying this ritual is not going online. You can use your computer if you just need to write. Spend time savouring a cup of tea or coffee and read. You can meditate, do yoga, take a walk or sit quietly and do nothing.

*start of the day: begin your day by starting a simple to do list with the 3 most important tasks (MIT). This will help you focus on what's important.

During the day, with all the distractions going on, do a refocus ritual which will only take a minute or two. Close your browser or disconnect during this time and maybe take a walk to get your blood circulating. Before you consider going online or to use social media, look again at your to-do list and what you need to accomplish.

*alternate focus and rest: make it a ritual to alternate between focus and rest and your use of social media or communicate first and then create blocks of focus.

An example is to set a timer and give yourself 45 minutes to do your email, Twitter, Facebook IM and any other reading. Then either be disciplined not to use the internet or social media and use the next few hours to focus on being productive and creating. Gradually start to reduce the amount of time you spend on social media.

*at the end of the day: review what you have done and think about how you could improve. Consider disconnecting for the rest of the evening and think about what you will focus on tomorrow.

*do a weekly focus ritual: Review your week and projects to make sure that you are still on track.

- **Overcome the need for instant gratification and speed**

As we continue to use technology, which is fast, response immediate and gratifying, we are attuning our minds, bodies and emotions to be in sync with that, but we are not computers and therefore we need to overcome the need for speed and doing things quickly and in the process hastily. We need to take time to do what we need to do. Slowing down has the benefits of allowing us to focus better, appreciate things better, more enjoyment and reduces the stress.

Don't you enjoy a meal more if you eat it slowly or spend time with a friend or to read a book? How different is it if you do these things hurriedly? Once you have freed up some time from using social media, you will realise how much time you actually have-which is a lot to do all the things your heart desires.

- **Let go of the need to stay updated**

The fear of missing out is a symptom of wanting to keep updated. It's because we are afraid we will either miss something important or an opportunity. You need to change your mind-set that you are not missing out.

- **Identify the emotional need you are trying to fill**

Each time you log onto social network, you are feeding into your emotional needs, consciously or unconsciously. You either bored, curious, feeling tired, lonely or stressed.

Just think about it, once you log on and an hour later of surfing in Twittersphere or Facebook world, what have you gained. Has the loneliness changed, do you feel happier or less stressed. There's no evidence to support these changes, and in fact as you have read, there's evidence to suggest that it could be making you depressed, lonelier, affecting your concentration, increasing your stress levels and impacting on other areas in your life.

- **Create an uncluttered environment**

In order to be more productive and less distracted, create an environment at your work or home that's clutter free. It could be from playing soothing, relaxing music, to having nice pictures on the walls. This will create the ambience of less distraction and reduce the itch to check your gadgets.

- **Get close support**

If you have difficulty in doing any of this, speak to a friend, partner or family member to help you manage your account. With some support and assistance from someone else, eventually you will be able to have more control of your life and your social network activity. This will also ensure that you are not neglecting your other pursuits. You could also go to the extreme to change your password and give them access to it and you only log on when you are with them.

- **Disable email notifications**

Disabling email notifications will help as you won't be tempted or distracted by a notification that you have a facebook message or a tweet. It will automatically reduce that itch, urge and compulsive checking of your social media account.

- **Install the Facebook Demetricator**

I heard about this in November 2014, an application by Ben Gosser

If you haven't seen it yet, the Demetricator is a browser extension that removes all the overt quantification from your experience of Facebook. That means that red bulb which flashes the numbers which attracts you to log on and stay on facebook gets removed. With Facebook Demetricator installed and toggled ON, it doesn't matter if 2, 20, or 20,000 people like your most recent status update (for example); when you view that status update, you see simply "people like this." Visit someone's profile, and you see that they have "Friends"—not "Friends 450" or "Friends 4,500." "View all 6 comments" becomes "View all comments," and "*n* hours ago" becomes either "recently" or "a while ago."

Grosser explains that,

"As a regular user of Facebook I continually find myself being enticed by its endless use of numbers. How many likes did my photos get today? What's my friend count? How much did people like my status? I focus on these quantifications, watching for the counts of responses rather than the responses themselves, or waiting for numbers of friend requests to appear rather than looking for meaningful connections. In other words, these numbers lead me to evaluate my participation within the system from a metricated viewpoint."

- **Unplug totally or use blocking software**

If you feel you need to, you could unplug for that duration that you have decided to be offline or use software to block certain sites from your computer i.e. there are software designed to block twitter and facebook.
You can use Leech block which blocks specific sites in Firefox and stay focused which allows you to choose which sites you want to block.

- **Curb impulsive checking and live in the moment**

If you are at a party, and in a group, and few people are looking on their mobiles, and you are compelled to whip out your phone. Think before doing this and choose to talk to someone and enjoy the moment of being at the party, actually enjoying the party and feeling that your presence is physically there and nowhere else. If you're in a queue at the supermarket, just try smiling and enjoying that moment, without whipping out your devices. Look around you and become more aware of what's going on and who's around you.

- **Leave your mobile device behind or shut it off**

If you're on the go, you don't always need to be connected. Sure having our iPhone, Blackberry or Android is cool to have, but having them on us, with rings, dings and pings later just feed into our addictions. If you know you are not expecting anything important and it can wait a while, put your phone on silent if you are meeting someone, going out with family or turn it off. It will give you an opportunity to enjoy what you are doing and connect with the person, and give them your undivided attention. Just imagine you are on the receiving of someone who is preoccupied and distracted every few minutes checking their phone, or who is using their later facebook or tweet to make a conversation. That's so not cool I think, and not sure why we think it's acceptable, and the person on the receiving end has to endure it without saying a word.

- **Disconnect after work**

If its work stuff that keeps you distracted, become disciplined to draw a line, that after 5pm, no work at home and use this time to spend with yourself, friends and family.

- **Think before you click…**

Each time you are compelled to update your status, skim, surf and tweet, ask yourself, what am I gaining from this interaction of sending this picture, tweeting or updating my status?

When you log on, depending on what else you are doing or could be doing, think to yourself, what am I gaining out of this? Just imagine what else you could be doing in that time for example, reading, going out with a friend, catching up with family or going to the gym.

- **Incorporate time for other activities**

Once you have gradually reduced your time in social media world, you would have freed up some of your time. Try to then occupy your time and incorporate time to do other things you enjoy doing, whether it is going to a movie, for coffee, dinner, or calling a friend. Maybe also think of going to the gym or exercising, meditating, do yoga daily and of course eat healthily. Some people find also that they neglect their chores because of their social network use. If you have spare time, consider using this to complete your chores. Make it a habit also, to take time out to do something good for someone else, like buying a bunch of flowers or helping out a friend that needs help with something.

Some people also neglect their appearance and grooming. Consider spending more time on yourself, grooming and your appearance rather than spending all your time on social media, which if you're overweight, or struggling with low self-esteem is going to make your feel even worse.

Start with simple basic stuff like keeping your hair tidy, shaving if you have to and love yourself enough to look your best. Spoil yourself with an hour long massage, manicure or pedicure- things that you don't do because you never thought you had time for.

- **Go outside**.

There are limitless benefits of being in nature and just soaking in the fresh air, being in sunshine or enjoying the breeze on a sandy beach. There is evidence to support that being in nature is healing. Think about the next time you are having a lunch break or free time, to leave your devices behind and go for a walk, run, bike ride or just enjoy being in nature. Take time out to recharge your batteries.

- **Reclaim your circadian sleep wake cycle**

A lot of people who are addicted to internet or social media have disturbed sleeping patterns. It's important therefore to monitor your mood and sleep. As you begin to reduce the time you spend, you will notice an improvement in your energy levels and also an improvement in your sleep pattern. This will also ensure that you are not tired during the day, and thus improve your concentration and memory. Look at your sleep hygiene and consider what you need to change. If you have the habit of checking your accounts first thing in the morning and last thing at night, change it.

- **Set yourself SMART goals and follow your dreams**

The evidence suggest that lots of people that you interact with online are actually addicted to social network. In a sense, its people who are happy spending their time using social world. On the other hand for some people this time is precious and they would rather use it to pursue their ambitions. Write yourself specific, measurable, and achievable, realistic and time limited goals (SMART) –and also consider learning something new, like learning a new dance like salsa, playing an instrument, a new language, yoga or a sport like tennis or squash.

- **Retrain your brain**

If you have been a user of social media, as you have read earlier your neurons and neural pathways would have been conditioned to the email notifications, the rings, and pings and dings our phones make when we get a tweet or message.

You will have to learn to retrain the circuits in your brains to avoid being distracted and impulsive. This will come with time, but it's about replacing your social media use with activities which are more meaningful and add value to your life. For example opt for real socializing and strengthen these neural pathways which would be beneficial in the long run.

If you want to take it a step further, what all these suggestions above lead you to, is for you to consider seriously to go on an internet cleanse/detox/diet/sabbatical:

In order to accomplish this, identify the other streams of distraction other than social media.

Using social media is one thing, but with lots of blogs, businesses and forums all connected to social media, the stream of distraction that we face in our days is enormous. If you work online, this could also be a challenge.

Some examples of distractions are:
Email, instant messaging, Twitter, Facebook, online forums, blogs, other social networks, new sites, mobiles, text messages, skype, podcasts, google alerts, mobile device notifications, mobile apps, online music, online shopping, videos and YouTube, internet radio, online games , internet TV, eBooks and so much more.

With all these connections, there is just so much distraction. You don't want to reduce your social network use and fill it up with other distractions.

Consider starting a cleanse from the stream of distraction:
It's a good idea to go on a cleanse from the stream of distraction. It can be scary to do this, so start with going on a mini cleanse for just half a day or a whole day and then on to longer periods. We might not realise it but we need to give our brains some downtime.

Steps in a cleanse:
*Don't check email or other types of digital inboxes.
*Don't log into Facebook, Twitter or other social networks.
*Don't read news, blogs or subscriptions.
*Don't check your favourite websites.
*Use your phones for as little time as possible.
*Change your mind-set that you don't need to respond immediately and create response free zone.
*Spend time creating, working on important projects, getting outside, communicating with people and exercising.
*Spend your time reading books.

Attempt to set yourself a goal of doing it once a week and then consider more times to cleanse. Once you start to do this, you will realise the benefits and value of doing this.

Have you notice when you are online, the compulsion to take in information. Start to be selective of what you choose to read and how much value it is making to your life and in your self-growth.

Despite all this, you cannot simply consider changing. Some of you reading this might think it's unrealistic to even consider the prospect of deteching or reducing their social network use. It could be that your work doesn't allow it, or that it's your only form of socialising.

If you have to use social network for work purposes, that's fine, be introspective as to how much has it helped your business. Steve Pavlina researched this before stopped his use of social networks and came to the conclusion that facebook and twitter was just creating traffic, but not necessarily linked to sales. Companies are going to have to consider the time their employees spend on social networks especially as there's evidence out there that it's decreasing productivity.

You can still take responsibility for your work and your life and limit the time you spend on social media. Speak to your employer to discuss the changes you are making to either slow things down or to incorporate slots in the day to be productive.

- **Be aware of withdrawal symptoms and seek professional help**
As you have been alluded to, giving up or curbing your addiction comes with withdrawal symptoms. When you start to feel anxious, craving, miserable, and jittery and feels like losing control, maybe you could seek professional help and support.

- **Use other forms of communication**
It's amazing when you realise that actually there are other forms of communication. If it's someone's birthday, send them a card. Make the effort of calling them and getting them a present. Call a friend, family member or colleague instead of sending them a text. If you're on holiday, take photographs and actually have them developed to be put into an album, which you can then share with those close to you. Make someone's day and do something good for someone. One idea of mine is have a box of all the things that you will need i.e. cards, thank you notes, post its, gift bags as this will make it easier for you to do. If you have kids, let them get used to getting involved in writing and actually knowing about simple things like birthday cards, post cards, gifts, and thank you notes.

- **Build relationships**
Focus on the relationships and those close to you. As you have seen, the relationships in social media is not real. Make the effort of rekindling those relationships you lost through social network. Find other ways of socialising. Go out with friends instead of chatting online. Go for a movie, to the park or out with family.

- **Use privacy settings to ensure you are not being targeted by others**
If you continue to use social media, then use privacy settings which are

available. We have seen already that the effect of privacy settings are very important in order for you to safeguard your profile and those who have access to it.

- **Seek professional help**

Professionals like psychiatrists, psychologists, nurses, mental health workers and paediatricians are in a unique position to educate families about both the complexities of the digital world and the challenging social and health issues that online youth experience. Families are being encouraged to face the core issues of bullying, popularity status, depression, social anxiety, risk-taking and sexual development."

In severe cases, you might need to have help in the form of being admitted into an internet rehabilitation clinics. There are now several clinics being set up worldwide in United Kingdom, USA, Japan and the rest of the world. One such clinic, Restart, in Washington, are teaching meditation and mindfulness in the UK. Another Priory hospital in Roehampton, United Kingdom, rehab program consists of 3 parts of CBT, psychodynamic psychotherapy and social behaviour adjustments. Other forms of treatment include going cold turkey from electronic devices and learning social skills like face to face contact.

The main focus is on psychological or talking treatments. As mentioned previously, mindfulness is the new buzz word.

Start to practice Mindfulness

Mindfulness experts like Shamash Alidina from learnmindfulness. co.uk, are teaching people the following principles to achieve mindfulness in the 21st century:
• Live in the now and concentrate on the present moment.
• When you get up in the morning instead of whipping out and checking your emails, tweets and Facebook IM, concentrate on the moment and your breathing, devoid of technological distractions.

Practice gratitude
• Another principle is to spend time to write down 5 things you are most grateful for.

Practice savouring
• Emphasis is also to train yourself to tune into your senses, to connect with the smells, sights and sounds around you rather than filling your time with technology-something which is called savouring.

Practice being in the flow
• Another mindfulness instructor Michael Chaskalson from mbsr.co.uk, explains that in life, it is all about 'flow'. This means that you need to be fully engage with what you are doing.
• He emphasizes that you should show up for your life every day and regularly ask yourself, what's happening around me right now that I'm missing?
• Next time you're multi-tasking, ask yourself what I am getting from this? If it's laughter, support or knowledge, continue. If it's just killing time then de-tech.

I am certain that Mindfulness will be able to help in the milder cases of addiction however, in the more severe cases, as it is an addiction and affecting the dopamine levels and other neurotransmitters or chemicals in our brains, then medication will be needed to be considered. This might be especially for conditions like depression, OCD, anxiety and eating disorders.

For parents and the younger generations
The most affected generations are the younger generation. You have read Jo Frosts warning. They are growing up in an era where it's alright to have 500-1000 friends of different age groups whether these are real or not, it doesn't matter. Their era of being consumed by social media as you have read earlier are robbing them of opportunities of fulfilling their dreams. They are living lives of being totally distracted and not being able to cope with their studies or perform to their best ability.

• Setting an example
The children of the world are our future and therefore parents are crucial in tackling these disorders as they need to set an example. Children will model their parents and peers. If children are seeing their parents using their mobile or iPad every few minutes, then they will model this behaviour and feel that this behaviour is normal and acceptable.

Clearly we as adults owe it to them and the future generations to tackle this problem before it affects their future. Why should our children be robbed of the richness in relationships, studies and lives that we have had? I am so grateful for the opportunities I have had without the technology and continue to do so, as I spend time with my children in the outdoors, in parks, on holidays, free from distraction. Ultimately it's a choice each person has to make.

I feel I have been fortunate to be able to go to the library and take my children to a library to soak in the experience and richness of the experience and knowledge that is available on shelves. There's clearly no comparison in reading a book, with the smell of a new book, and flicking of the pages, in comparison with an eBook.

How fortunate have we been to be able to have time and take time to learn and study without distractions which children face today. I remember preparing in advance to study, making notes, and reading from textbooks to ensure I was prepared for my medical exams. As parents we have the responsibility to mould the future for them and show them the right way.

• Open the avenues of communication
As a parent, open the lines of communication with your child. **This is what Jo Frost has advised that parents open the dialogues of communication.** If you take the time to communicate with them you will be able to build a trusting relationship with them.

• Net negotiation
Negotiate or come to an agreement as to realistic amount of time they need to spend on social network. There is a time and place for gadgets and using social network and therefore relay this message to your child. Let them have set times when they can use their mobiles. Also reward positive behaviour for example if they do their homework, then they can have time if you felt they deserved to.

• Spend time with them doing activities or going out
It's amazing when I spend time with my children as to how they appreciate the little things, whether it's painting with them, playing pickup sticks, just reading a book or taking them out to parks and taking them out for hot chocolate. There are so many games that you can play without using

technology, so think about getting started with spending quality of time with them and making the effort to do so. Children are our future so time spent with them is well worth the investment.

The road to recovery and wellbeing for social media users
The journey and road to any addiction is not by any means easy, but the fact that you are reading this book and attempting to consider changing your use of social media is the step in the right direction towards your ultimate recovery and wellbeing. I feel I would have succeeded even if you have just read and have an awareness of the psychological effects that social media is having on each of us as individuals.

As you have read, the addiction has been described as any other addiction like the addiction to drug use, which as we know is difficult to treat.

I know social media is here to stay and it is still going to influence our lives in the future, and therefore, it is about taking control of our own lives and how we want social media to influence it. Another key message is that we have created technology to influence us in the way it has, and therefore ultimately despite external influences and temptations we need to take control of it and not the other way around.

The next few pages has a 30 day plan of the HEART guide for social media to get you started if you have realised and accepted that you need to do something about your social media use.

HEART for Social media detox
Happily ever active recovery tool for social media detox ©Seshni
Social network CBT ©

Sample

Weekday	Time on social media	No of times checking gadgets or having itch to do	Time for activities Exercise, leisure, Calling someone	Effect on mood Sleep energy levels	Long term goals	Withdrawal Symptoms- Craving, compulsion, Checking, anxiety, jittery, losing control ,FOMO
Monday	Am Pm Evening					
Tuesday	Am Pm Evening					
Wednesday	Am Pm Evening					
Thursday	Am Pm Evening					
Friday	Am Pm Evening					
Saturday	Am Pm Evening					
Sunday	Am Pm Evening					

HEART for Social media detox
Happily ever active recovery tool for social media detox ©Seshni

Social network CBT ©

Sample

Weekday	Time on social media	No of times checking gadgets or having itch to do	Time for activities Exercise, leisure, Calling someone	Effect on mood Sleep energy levels	Long term goals	Withdrawal Symptoms- Craving, compulsion, Checking, anxiety, jittery, losing control ,FOMO
Monday	Am Pm Evening					
Tuesday	Am Pm Evening					
Wednesday	Am Pm Evening					
Thursday	Am Pm Evening					
Friday	Am Pm Evening					
Saturday	Am Pm Evening					
Sunday	Am Pm Evening					

HEART for Social media detox
Happily ever active recovery tool for social media detox ©Seshni

Social network CBT ©

Sample

Weekday	Time on social media	No of times checking gadgets or having itch to do	Time for activities Exercise, leisure, Calling someone	Effect on mood Sleep energy levels	Long term goals	Withdrawal Symptoms- Craving, compulsion, Checking, anxiety, jittery, losing control ,FOMO
Monday	Am Pm Evening					
Tuesday	Am Pm Evening					
Wednesday	Am Pm Evening					
Thursday	Am Pm Evening					
Friday	Am Pm Evening					
Saturday	Am Pm Evening					
Sunday	Am Pm Evening					

HEART for Social media detox
Happily ever active recovery tool for social media detox ©Seshni

Social network CBT ©

Sample

Weekday	Time on social media	No of times checking gadgets or having itch to do	Time for activities Exercise, leisure, Calling someone	Effect on mood Sleep energy levels	Long term goals	Withdrawal Symptoms-Craving, compulsion, Checking, anxiety, jittery, losing control ,FOMO
Monday	Am Pm Evening					
Tuesday	Am Pm Evening					
Wednesday	Am Pm Evening					
Thursday	Am Pm Evening					
Friday	Am Pm Evening					
Saturday	Am Pm Evening					
Sunday	Am Pm Evening					

CHAPTER THIRTEEN

Predictions for the future.

"We must accept finite disappointment, we must never look infinite hope."

Martin Luther King

So having delved into the good, the not so good, the glamorous and amazing opportunities these networks have given us, we are back to the beginning. Has Mark Zuckerberg, and Jack Horsey created the alpha and the omega of things….Or looking at the facets of Pandora's Box, which has been unleashed, are we sure that the amazing effects it's given us, and the beastly facet, doesn't matter as there is so much more that we are benefitting.

Can we continue to put our fate in the hands of the digital age, and are we ready for it? Looking at how much has transpired from Facebook to Twitter to YouTube, are we ready for what's next, or is it that looking 10 or 20 years down the road, and at our timelines, that we think that maybe we should have not unleashed the beast.

There are no rights or wrongs, there is no right or wrong time, the key message and wisdom that is being offered to us, is in the clues that Mark Zuckerburg's original intent which was to make the world a more better and connected place, and that if we are able to control this then the world would be a more better place for us to live in.

I have no doubt that there are huge positives and that this connection is making our worlds a better place, but he is saying we can control this, but this is not the case.

There is no means of control when someone else decides to divulge your secrets or that you should have been at work and you were not. There is no control when you are fired because of something your employers found out through your profiles…so how then do we control it, or do we continue to be immersed in this matrix.

Well that is for another guide of pearls of wisdom of choosing to live in the now, and becoming the master and not a slave to the digital age which we appear to be. We have a choice in everything we do, and therefore we can choose what we want to do, whether we want to be engulfed by technology and embrace it with full force, and head on, despite the fears of the unknown potential and effects it can have or do we want to take control and live in the now and choose how to use the magic of technology in your life wiser.

So 10 years down the line, and having explored the various features of Facebook, its addictive nature and its effect on our psyche we end back at the beginning so we are back to where we started. Somewhat wiser. If we look back to the beginning of where this all started, on a college campus. Therefore it is not surprising that this still has one of the greatest impact on our college students and campuses around the world.

Where are those days when children would go out to play, ride their bicycle and enjoy the connection of friends at a playground? These carefree and cherished moments are now being traded for the laptop screen or mobile phone.

The effects on the younger generation is showing no doubt that it has its greatest influence and therefore this is the area of concern. There are everyday concern that Facebook and Twitter and psychological effects are adversely affecting lives of these younger generation and adults. The only person that makes this decision of either enjoying everyday interaction and moments is you, and you can live in a world with Facebook or any other social networking like Twitter and still enjoy those brief pleasures of life and what life experiences has to offer.

Is the social network good or bad? This is a complex question to answer. Despite attempts by media, governments, organisations and our protests, social media is now a vital part of life and is here to stay!!

The key message is that academia needs to learn to take effective advantage of this. When social media is integrated into academics it has shown serious positive effect on students.

The predictions for the future are that Facebook and Twitter will actually part of the site of the internet controlling more than we can now imagine. That's not surprising as now businesses, blogs, etc. are all part of this social networking, which begs us to answer the question I initially started which was …to be on Facebook, Twitter and other social networks or not?

It's true that Facebook and Twitter can lead to a false sense of connection to faraway friends, since few members post about the true difficulties of their lives. But most of us still know, despite Facebook's abuse of what should be the holiest word in the language, that a news feed full of constantly updating "friends," like a room full of chattering people, is no substitute for a face to face conversation.

Indeed, so much of what has made these worthwhile comes from the site's provisions for both hiding and sharing. It is not hard to draw the conclusion that some things shouldn't be "shared" at all, but rather said, whether through e-mail, instant message, text message, Facebook's own "private message" system, or over the phone, or with a cup of coffee, or beside a pitcher of beer.

I guess my readers, Facebookers or non Facebookers, tweeters or non-tweeters, that only time will tell, and I hope that 10 years down the line, that we will not be looking at our Facebook and Twitter profiles and dread or regret the choices, messages, wall, etc. that we made…

I guess if we bear in the mind the initial purpose of what it is meant for is to connect and share our lives with the people that matter the most to us. Not the so called 1000 or so friends.

The future for Facebookers and tweeters is that our lives, if you so choose do be a Facebooker or tweeter, is that you will become dependent. It will be something that will control your life, if that is something that you wish to do.

Like all things in life, it's irrelevant or whether this is good or bad for us. If the purpose of what Facebook and Twitter was created was for connecting people and making this a more open world, then I admit that it might be something which is for purpose of good.

However what no one, not even Mark Zuckerberg or Jack Dorsey can predict is what the future holds. I guess there will always be the fear of the unknown like everything in life. So does this mean that you remain constantly in fear or do you like the 1.19 billion people around the globe succumb to the social networking site?

Whilst Facebook may own the rights to your profile and everything else that you have on your Facebook account, I think that we each have some degree of control of our Facebook and Twitter account, and that ultimately, you are the only one who can make that decision of either using it wisely, balancing your life in the cyber world and the real world or you have a choice of becoming dependent and addicted to Facebook. You can either join it or be against it. You can let it work for you or you can be its slave. The choice ultimately is yours to make. There are definitely some elements of the social networking that are good and there are some that are not so good.

Like all things in life, it's about striking that balance. Facebook and Twitter is here, and it's here to stay, and the predictions for the future are that it's going to have more control over our lives and the world around us, and in a sense Mark Zuckerberg would have succeeded in making this a more open world in connecting our real lives with the cyber world.

I conclude with the question I set out with which is to be or not to be on Facebook or Twitter…are we any wiser knowing what we do about social networking …and do we want to make it the alpha and omega of our lives. What do we think is the future for generation z and alpha-the glass generation? Do we think the new social network like the smiley face 'ello' will be able to catch up seeing that they are saying that you are not a product and it's simple, beautiful and ad-free…let's wait and see

My penultimate message to you reader is *'think before you click', live in the now and claim your Twitter and Facebook freedom.*

MY STORY
"I know I am happy being tweet and Facebook free. I am living in the now, I am enjoying the richness of experiences and adventures. I savour every experience using all my senses. I know I am not missing out and I am loving every minute of it without the distractions of the rings, dings and pings."

Thanks a million for reading my book …

Further reading and information

GENERATION TYPES
Greatest Generation (born 1901-1943)
Silent generation or traditionalist, radio babies Markers- World War 2. The greatest depression, advent of television and telephone.

Baby boomers (1943-1964)
The me generation.

Generation X (1963-1980)
First generation of Latchkey kids.
Markers-first generation to embrace the personal computer and internet. Techno-literal.

Generation Y- Millennial (born 1977-2000)
Markers technology /menu driven society.
They were the first to grow up with computers. Their world has always had computers. Technological savvy generation using interactive media instant messaging, text, messaging, blogs, and multi-player games.

Generation Z (born 1995-2012)
First generation never to experience the pre internet world. Technologically focused and iPad generation

Generation Alpha (born 2010)
Google kids whose toys that require electric or batteries. The prediction for this generation is that they will be digitally wired up requiring 24/7 connectivity.

SOCIAL NETWORK GLOSSARY

BBM
Instant messaging on blackberry handsets.

Connectome
Project looking into the hubs of connection in our brain.

Divided attention disorder
Disorder in which a person is constantly distracted by social media and technological devices.

Digitalised
Choosing to use technology in your daily life.

Facebook
Literally an online book of faces.

Facebook addiction disorder
Disorder characterised by an intense addiction to spending excessive time on social media Facebook.

Facebook and Twitter graveyards
Virtual cemeteries of deceased social network users.

Facebook depression
Depressive disorder caused by using Facebook. It causes decreased self-esteem and the need to compare oneself to others and to be popular.

Fear of missing out
People who when not on social media, start to experience the genuine fear that they are missing out if not logged on.

Food porn
It is a glamourized spectacular visual representation of cooking or eating in advertisements, infomercials, cooking shows or other visual media, foods boasting a high fat and calorie content. It takes on the form of food photography and styling.

Internet addiction disorder
Addiction to the internet.

IPAD
Apple device used for Internet.

IPOD
Apple device used to download music.

Media hub
Living rooms transformed with gadgets ranging from mobiles, computers, laptops, iPads and iPods.

Media mesh
Media meshing using social network to communicate on a related activity.

Media stacking
Media stacking using social media to communicate not related to activity.

Selfie
A photo taken of oneself to use on social media.

Selfitis
Obsession of taking selfies

Sexting
The act of sending sexually explicit messages primarily between mobile phones.

Social media
An instrument used for social communication.

Social media dependence syndrome
Syndrome characterised by the dependence to social media.

Status updates
Act of updating your social status on social networks with your personal information.

Texting
The act of sending messages between mobiles.

Tweets
Text messages limited to 140 characters.

Twitter
Social media using microblogging.

Twittering
Act of spending time on social media Twitter.

Twittourettes
The incessant need to send tweets.

Two screening
The act of surfing or browsing the internet on 2 display screens.

Techno Savvy
Millennial generation

WhatsApp
Free instant messaging on mobile devices.

Whatsappatitis
Addiction to using WhatsApp to send messages resulting in injury to your joints in your fingers.

YouTube
Site used to upload videos.

INDEX

Briton- 18
Business- 27, 36, 50, 52, 62, 89, 104, 121, 134, 150, 152
Butterfly effect- 72
Buzz – 12, 77, 79, 81, 98, 112, 153
Bytes- 25, 100

C
Caesar- 96
Celebrity- 8, 69, 71, 74
Celebrity lover- 9, 11, 88, 91
Charles Leadbeater- 71
Chelsea B- 5, 46
Click- 30, 42, 85, 96, 97, 99, 127, 128, 130, 136, 148
Collector- 85
College- 35, 45, 52, 61, 99, 101, 114, 121, 134, 173
College campus- 99, 134
Communication- 13, 17, 18, 20, 22, 26, 42, 55, 56, 66, 68, 70, 81, 97, 105, 118, 119, 138, 152, 155, 163
Community- 45, 46, 52, 81
Companion- 71, 97
Connection- 25, 31, 40, 51, 54, 55, 57, 68, 70, 74, 75, 79-81, 96, 98, 131, 133-135, 140, 151, 162
Connectome- 25, 79-81, 162
Courts- 51
Crimes- 50, 52
Cyberbullying- 8, 10, 25, 49, 64, 66, 110, 119, 122, 125
Cynic- 85

D
Daily user- 71
Daniel Radcliffe- 35
Data centric lives- 36
Death threats- 8-10, 63
Deepak Chopra- 54
Defriend- 44, 45
De-ja-vu- 9
Dependence- 12, 76, 99, 104, 108, 113, 120, 121, 123, 142, 145, 163
De-tech- 33, 98, 138, 139, 141, 154

Utopia- 74

ABOUT THE AUTHOR

Dr Seshni Moodliar is a psychiatrist who has specialised in people with Intellectual Disabilities, having also trained in the various specialities of psychiatry. She has a keen interest in perinatal psychiatry, addictions, Autism, ADHD and mental health wellbeing and recovery.

She is also the author of Pass the CASC, a book used by psychiatrists worldwide for their membership exams with the Royal College of Psychiatry and also author of Core psychiatric interview skills.